COLLECTOR'S
VALUE GUIDE™

Department 56®
Villages

The Heritage Village Collection®
The Original Snow Village®

Secondary Market Price Guide
& Collector Handbook

FOURTH EDITION

Department 56® Villages

This publication is *not* affiliated with Department 56®, Inc. or any of its affiliates, subsidiaries, distributors or representatives. Any opinions expressed are solely those of the authors, and do not necessarily reflect those of Department 56®, Inc. The Heritage Village Collection®, The Original Snow Village®, Dickens' Village®, New England Village®, Christmas in the City® and Storybook Village® are registered trademarks of Department 56®, Inc. Alpine Village Series™, North Pole Series™, Disney Park Villages™, Little Town of Bethlehem™ and Historical Landmark Series™ are trademarks of Department 56®. Charles Dickens' Signature Series© and the American Architecture Series© are copyrights of Department 56. Product names and product designs are the property of Department 56®, Inc., Eden Prairie, MN. Photographs by CheckerBee, Inc.

Front cover (left to right): "Fire Station #3," The Original Snow Village; "The University Club," *Christmas in the City.*

Back cover (left to right): "Dash Away Delivery," *North Pole*; "Norman Church," *Dickens' Village*; "Adobe House," The Original Snow Village.

Managing Editor:	Jeff Mahony	Art Director:	Joe T. Nguyen
Associate Editors:	Melissa A. Bennett	Production Supervisor:	Scott Sierakowski
	Jan Cronan	Senior Graphic Designers:	Carole Mattia-Slater
	Gia C. Manalio		Leanne Peters
	Paula Stuckart	Graphic Designers:	Jennifer J. Denis
Contributing Editor:	Mike Micciulla		Lance Doyle
Editorial Assistants:	Jennifer Filipek		Sean-Ryan Dudley
	Nicole LeGard Lenderking		Kimberly Eastman
	Joan C. Wheal		Ryan Falis
Research Assistants:	T.R. Affleck		Jason C. Jasch
	Priscilla Berthiaume		David S. Maloney
	Heather N. Carreiro		David Ten Eyck
	Beth Hackett	Art Intern:	Janice Evert
	Victoria Puorro		
	Steven Shinkaruk		
Web Reporters:	Samantha Bouffard		
	Ren Messina		

ISBN 1-888914-48-3

CheckerBee
PUBLISHING

(formerly Collectors' Publishing)
306 Industrial Park Road • Middletown, CT 06457

TABLE OF CONTENTS

TABLE OF CONTENTS

INTRODUCING THE COLLECTOR'S VALUE GUIDE™

*W*elcome to the fourth edition of the Collector's Value Guide™ to Department 56® Villages. Inside this book you'll find tons of great information about the wonderful lighted buildings that have grown from a holiday tradition to a year-round craze.

We've divided the book between Heritage Village, Snow Village and Other Department 56 Collectibles; with all the sections having their own overview, descriptions of new  releases and Value Guide sections. Within each Value Guide section, the buildings and accessories are pictured in color, along with essential information such as stock number, issue and retirement dates (unless current), variations with secondary market values, the original price of the piece and what it is currently worth on the secondary market. Also, we've added two new villages, Storybook Village and Seasons Bay, the romantic resort town introduced this year.

Some exciting new sections have also been included in this year's book, such as an interview with Scott Enter, the designer of Snow Village buildings and accessories. You'll also read about how each building is carefully packaged for shipping and learn tips on how to arrange your buildings and accessories to create your own personal display. Plus, don't miss our fun "how-to" section on building your own display accents.

So, whether you are an experienced collector or a casual fan of any of the Department 56 villages, our Value Guide is filled with accurate, up-to-date information, as well as fun and informative sections that are sure to help you add a whole new level to your village hobby!

ℱ or more than 20 years, Department 56 has given its collectors continuous enjoyment through the lighted buildings it creates. Since the very first releases, collectors have enjoyed searching for pieces to add to their collections so that they can design the village of their dreams. And although the winter months and holiday season are often the most popular times for Department 56 displays, more and more collectors enjoy them throughout the year.

The history of Department 56 begins with in a small flower and garden shop in Minnesota. "Bachman's" started out as a family-owned farm in the late 1800s and began selling flowers during the early 1900s. Through the years, business flourished and, in the latter half of the 20th century, the shop branched out to take on giftware imports. The man responsible for this new "department," Ed Bazinet, eventually became the man behind the creation of Department 56 buildings.

In 1976, six lighted buildings were created to resemble a town with which Bazinet had fallen in love. The idea was to re-create the warm, quaint feeling of a small village right in your own home. It was these buildings that began "Snow Village." The houses were immediately popular and the division of Bachman's known as "Department 56" was soon on its way to becoming its own successful business. In fact, the demand for these these lighted buildings was so great, that three years after it's inception, Department 56 had its first retirement in an attempt to keep the collection to a manageable size. In 1983, to avoid confusion with a growing number of imitators, the line's name became "The Original Snow Village."

In 1984, another line of lighted buildings was introduced by Department 56. Inspired by the famous author Charles Dickens and the London of the Victorian era of which he wrote, *Dickens' Village* became an instant success with collectors.

In 1986, two new villages joined *Dickens' Village* under the heading of "Heritage Village." They were *New England Village* and *Alpine Village* and each featured a unique style of architecture typical to the region for which they were named. One year later, *Christmas in the City* was introduced along with *Little Town Of Bethlehem*, which remains the only village released in its entirety. Retirements began for *Dickens' Village* in 1989 and two years later, another village, *North Pole* was released, followed by *Disney Parks Village Series* in 1994.

SHOWROOM TOUR!

Department 56 opens their Minnesota showroom Friday afternoons in the summer months. For more information, please write or call:

Department 56
One Village Place
Showroom Tour
6436 City West Parkway
Eden Prairie, MN 55344
1-800-LIT-TOWN

With the villages' growing success, collectors began to want a way to share their love of collecting with others. Soon, local clubs began forming across the country and, to help unify collectors, the National Council of "56" Clubs was formed. Although the local clubs are not sponsored by Department 56, the company acknowledges and supports them. As a thank you for their dedication, Department 56 surprised club members with the "Collectors' Club House" (set/2), a piece made exclusively for club members.

In 1992, collectors got the opportunity to not only collect the buildings, but to also invest in the company itself when Department 56 joined forces with the New York investment company, Forstmann, Little & Co. Much to the interest of collectors, stock was offered to the public shortly after the transaction was complete.

*T*he Heritage Village collection began in 1984 with the introduction of *Dickens' Village.* Its title, however, did not come about until several years later, when additional villages were added, creating the need to name the entire collection. Today, seven villages make up Heritage Village and each brings its own unique "personality" to Department 56's stable of collectible villages.

DICKENS' VILLAGE

Dickens' Village replicates the nostalgia of the Charles Dickens' Victorian era. The village portrays the days of the English author through porcelain pubs, cottages and shops, bringing to life the London of long-ago. While most of the buildings are not factual, there are some that are directly related to Charles Dickens' life, including "Gad's Hill Place," his home until he died in the late 1800s.

The *Historic Landmark Series*, introduced in 1997, is part of *Dickens' Village* and honors real-life historical buildings, such as "Big Ben" (set/2), where the young Dickens worked as a reporter, and "The Old Globe Theatre" (set/4). Other famous landmarks re-created in *Dickens' Village*, but not part of a series, include "Kenilworth Castle" and "Kensington Palace" (set/23), home of the late Princess Diana. Another series in the village, *Literary Classics*, which is new for 1999, honors the great novels of our times. The piece comes with a copy of the book for which the piece was derived.

As series play a large part of the collection, it is interesting to note the two series which are no longer a part of the *Dickens' Village* lineup. *Charles Dickens' Signature Series* and *Christmas Carol Revisited* are without new releases for the coming season. Accessories also have had series as well, including *The Twelve Days Of Dickens' Village*, which is currently up to its eleventh release.

NEW ENGLAND VILLAGE

Looking to capture the feeling of an old-fashion holiday in the heart of the northern woods, Department 56 introduced *New England Village*. Made up of a set of seven buildings, the 1986 introductions were the perfect start to owning your own small town. Most of the structures had a rustic, yet elegant style and the quaint village soon became a favorite with collectors from all parts of the country.

The buildings that make up this collection range from rambling farmhouses and barns; to mills, general stores, fisheries and lighthouses. All of these structures are common in towns throughout New England and are captured in true form by Department 56, complete with the deep, rich colors and simple architecture favored by New Englanders. Even the accessories exemplify life in the Northeast, with village staples, such as lobster trappers, lumberjacks, farm animals and, perhaps what New England is best known for, a red covered bridge.

Over the past 13 years since its inception, *New England Village* has grown to include 56 buildings, all of which are the epitome of life in the snow-covered Northeast. To date, less than 20 of the lighted buildings are still currently available in retail stores. And with only a handful of these buildings readily available, each one may seem to be a challenge to obtain, but is nonetheless, a joy to possess (and display).

The new pieces for 1999 include "Deacon's Way Chapel," "Franklin Hook & Ladder Co.," "Harper's Farm" and "Moggin Falls General Store." These four lighted buildings, along with the six new accessories, promise to keep up with the spirit and tradition of Department 56's *New England Village*.

ALPINE VILLAGE

Straight from the Swiss Alps, *Alpine Village* brings to life a small, far-away European village, complete with everything from chalets to churches. All pieces are masterfully created by Department 56 in grand style, bringing a wintry mountain town to you – and you never have to leave the warmth of your own home!

Alpine Village was first introduced in 1986, the same year as *New England Village*. The first release for this village was made up of a single set of five buildings, most of which were small, rough-looking stores. *Alpine Village* is unique in many ways, including having the first music box in any of the villages. The "Silent Night" accessory is actually a music box and was introduced 1995. "St. Nikolaus Kirche" is another interesting building as it is a factual representation of the church where "Silent Night" was said to be first heard. Both pieces are also currently available in stores.

Alpine Village has recently become the home of several pieces representing both a famous fictional family and a character with whom we are all familiar: the von Trapp family and Heidi. New this year, "*The Sound Of Music*® von Trapp Villa" (set/5) portrays the family home from the classic movie, *The Sound Of Music* and is the first licensed piece for this village. The building goes along with last year's accessory "Climb Every Mountain," (set/4) taken from the holiday favorite. The second of the two buildings released for 1999 is "Heidi's Grandfather's House." The piece is complemented by last year's accessory release "Heidi And Her Goats" (set/4) as well.

CHRISTMAS IN THE CITY

First introduced in 1987 with just six buildings, this collection is for anyone who has ever dreamed of life in the big city during the holiday season. With windows adorned with elaborate decorations, carolers strolling the streets, holiday shoppers and couples taking carriage rides through the parks, this village is the perfect depiction of big city holiday festivities. The collection of 49 buildings transforms the busy, everyday life of downtown into the perfect place to shop, sip a cup of joe in a corner café or peer out at those below from your top-floor brownstone apartment.

Christmas in the City buildings are typical of those found in most cities and depict the many museums, first-rate restaurants, grand churches, corner stores and apartment buildings that are common in larger cities across the country. Every building in this village is at least two-stories tall and have the aged look of classic metropolitan architecture with wrought iron window gates, brick walls and narrow windows. Most importantly, all the buildings are only steps from the bustling city streets where the fun is never far-off. There may be no yards to play in, but this kind of living puts one in the middle of all the action.

The four new buildings to join the *Christmas in the City* collection for 1999 are "Old Trinity Church," "*Precinct 25 Police Station,*" "The University Club," and "The Wedding Gallery." One of the many interesting accessories released this year is the "1919 Ford® Model-T." This classic car is sure to become a favorite in the *Christmas in the City* collection as well.

NORTH POLE

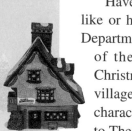

Have you ever wondered what Santa's house might look like or how his elves spend their time in the "off" season? Department 56's *North Pole* is the answer to these and many of the other pressing questions about the magic of Christmas. While *North Pole* remains one of the smaller villages, each building and accessory has its own unique characteristics, making this is a creative and fun addition to The Heritage Village Collection.

The *North Pole* began in 1990 and includes such buildings as the post office for all of Santa's mail and a greenhouse where Mrs. Claus likes to spend her free time (and perhaps earn some extra money selling Christmas trees?). The collection has recently grown to include over 40 buildings. This year, collectors get a glimpse of how Rudolph and the other reindeer learn to fly at "Reindeer Flight School." Also new for 1999, the "Real Plastic Snow Factory" gives collectors an inside look at where one of their favorite Department 56 display accessories comes from.

Another new addition this year is a new neighborhood known as *Elf Land*. The series is made up of smaller pieces that revolve around the lives of Santa's many helpers, the elves. Three of the five new pieces for 1999 belong in *Elf Land*.

Through the years, many of the lighthearted and colorful accessories of the *North Pole* collection have portrayed Santa and the elves both at work and at play. Lucky for them, it's hard to tell which one they do more often.

DISNEY PARKS VILLAGE SERIES

Department 56 graciously saluted the wonderful and magical world of Disney with its *Disney Parks Village Series,* a collection with a very short and unique history. It began in 1994 with the introduction of just four pieces. One year later, two more buildings were added. Then, in 1996, just two years after being released, the entire collection was retired at once. The retirement came as a surprise to collectors, who found the pieces quite difficult to find after the announcement.

Buildings that were a part of the *Disney Parks Village Series* were first sold at Disney World in Florida and Disney Land in California. The pieces in this series were meant to bring the experiences and memories of visiting the two theme parks into the homes of its guests.

LITTLE TOWN OF BETHLEHEM

Only 12 pieces make up this collection . . . and that includes buildings *and* accessories. Introduced in 1987 as a complete set, this nativity consists of only three buildings and several small accessories. This collection is still currently available.

*H*eritage Village continues to grow with 23 buildings released for 1999: eight in *Dickens' Village*, four for *New England Village*, two in *Alpine Village*, four in *Christmas in the City* and five in *North Pole*. Many new accessories, ornaments and hinged boxes were also added to the collection as well.

Dickens' Village

BIG BEN (SET/2) . . . As the most famous clock in the world, this grand structure adds the perfect touch to the *Historical Landmark Series*. The clock on the front of the tower is real and tells time when plugged in, while the other three clocks are set at 5:55. The tower and main structure are adorned with Christmas wreaths and garland enhancing the Christmas spirit in *Dickens' Village*.

GREAT EXPECTATIONS SATIS MANOR (SET/4) . . . This piece was inspired by the famed novel by Charles Dickens and is the first of the *Literary Classics* series. Overgrown trees and vines, crumbling walls and a ramshackle roof brings to life the house of Miss Havisham. Miss Havisham, perched in her oversized chair, along with Pip and Estella, complement this introductory piece.

HEATHMOOR CASTLE (LE-1999) . . . This limited edition castle is a reminder of the old days of Scotland. A banner reading "Heathmoor Castle" sways above the front door where the coat of arms is proudly displayed, while banners hang beside each of the windows. A spiral staircase leads to the door on the opposite side of the castle and gargoyles surround the top, warding off evil spirits.

THE HORSE AND HOUNDS PUB . . . The English tradition of drinking fine ale goes hand-in-hand with the tradition of fox hunting and there's no better building to exemplify this than "The Horse And Hounds Pub." The red and green brick building features a picture of a horse on the roof and lanterns on the sides sure to light up the night for the master and his riders to find their way after a long hunt.

LYNTON POINT TOWER . . . On those dreary nights that are so common in England, "Lynton Point Tower" helps the seamen of *Dickens' Village* find their way home. The light-keeper's house is perched high above the cold waters and the lighthouse stands tall beside it, shining a working light. "Lynton Point Tower" is the first lighthouse introduced in *Dickens' Village*.

NORTH EASTERN SEA FISHERIES LTD. . . . The day's haul comes off the fishing boats and right to the docks of the "North Eastern Sea Fisheries Ltd." Stands on the side of the building allow fish peddlers to sell the catch of the day, which can be anything from salmon to cod to herring – all of which would surely make a wonderful family feast.

TATTYEAVE KNOLL . . . While it could be considered by some to be a run-down shack, most people of Dickens' era would consider "Tattyeave Knoll" to be a "well-lived-in" cottage with personality. The lights shining from inside and the red bows around the front fence welcome all who come to visit. The sign above the front window signifies a town visited by characters from *Nicholas Nickleby*.

TEAMAN & CRUPP CHINA SHOP . . . One of the first things that comes to mind when thinking of London is fine tea. And what better way to enjoy your tea than to serve it in fine china from "Teaman & Crupp China Shop." The three-story shop offers the best selection anywhere in *Dickens' Village*.

DICKENS' VILLAGE ACCESSORIES . . . Eight singers celebrate the joyous season in the five-piece set **"HERE WE COME A-WASSAILING"** (set/5), while seven others spend their day **"SITTING IN CAMDEN PARK"** (set/4). A horse and rider clear a fence in **"ELEVEN LORDS A-LEAPING"** from the *The Twelve Days Of Dickens' Village* series. Friends say goodbye in **"UNTIL WE MEET AGAIN"** (set/2), while children roll their hoops in **"CHILD'S PLAY"** (set/2). **"ALE MATES"** (set/2) stop for a brief chat and a family gets ready for the spring growing season by **"TENDING THE COLD FRAME"** (set/3). This piece was also issued as a Bachman's exclusive.

All of the ornaments released this year are now lighted and battery-operated. Three of the new ornaments are re-releases: **"DICKENS' VILLAGE MILL," "DICKENS' VILLAGE CHURCH"** and **"THE OLD CURIOSITY SHOP."** The other, **"CHRISTMAS CAROL COTTAGES"** (set/3) includes: **"THE COTTAGE OF BOB CRATCHIT & TINY TIM," "FEZZIWIG'S WAREHOUSE"** and **"SCROOGE & MARLEY COUNTING HOUSE."**

Two hinged boxes were also added to the 1999 *Dickens' Village* line. The driver of the **"ROYAL COACH"** guides his horse to pick-up Her Majesty, while in **"SLEIGHRIDE"** a boy in his ice skates pulls his sweetheart in a one-person sleigh.

NEW ENGLAND VILLAGE

DEACON'S WAY CHAPEL . . . Grand churches similar to the "Deacon's Way Chapel" can be found throughout New England. This luminous chapel is soft blue in color and has large red doors in front to welcome guests. Many of the buildings characteristics are typical of churches in the North such as a stone foundation, a round stained-glass window and a tiered steeple. This particular church was built in 1849, as noted by the sign that hangs above the front door.

FRANKLIN HOOK & LADDER CO. . . . Constructed of stone on the first floor and wood on the second floor, "Franklin Hook & Ladder Co." is the perfect addition to rustic *New England Village*. A bell in the tower alerts the crew when there's a fire, while a water tower in the back of the firehouse gives the firemen plenty of water when needed and large doors provide a quick exit when time is of the essence. The front of the building is beautifully decorated with garland, bows and wreaths, adding a festive touch for the holiday season.

HARPER'S FARM . . . The front of "Harper's Farm" has been turned into a business where the townspeople of *New England Village* go to get their fresh fruits, vegetables and dairy products. The large sign above the door calls attention to the building so sight-seers driving by can come in and get a taste of the wares of a working New England farm.

MOGGIN FALLS GENERAL STORE . . . This is one store where you can get it all, from firewood to eggs to last minute preparations for holiday guests. An American flag flies on the right side of the building and a wreath hangs between the windows of the second floor. The "Moggin Falls General Store" has been around for years and is a common spot for locals to catch up on the daily news.

NEW ENGLAND VILLAGE ACCESSORIES . . . After a trip to the general store, a villager begins to **"LOAD UP THE WAGON"** (set/2). A man takes advantage of the holiday season; making a point of getting caught **"UNDER THE MISTLETOE"** with his sweetheart, while another is busy **"FLY-CASTING IN THE BROOK."** **"VOLUNTEER FIREFIGHTERS"** (set/2) practice their parts in the event of a real fire, while down at the **"FARMER'S MARKET"** (set/2), apples are today's special, with everything from apple cider to apple butter for sale. And, finally, a man puts the finishing touches on his work of art in **"AN ARTIST'S TOUCH."**

Three ornaments join *New England Village* this year, including **"CAPTAIN'S COTTAGE"** and **"STEEPLE CHURCH,"** which are new designs for 1999. **"CRAGGY COVE LIGHTHOUSE,"** however, is a re-release of a previous non-lit ornament.

ALPINE VILLAGE

HEIDI'S GRANDFATHER'S HOUSE . . . Inspired by the famed novel *Heidi*, this adorable house is a perfect fit in *Alpine Village*. "Heidi's Grandfather's House" is a cozy chalet, complete with a wooden exterior and overhanging roof, just as you would expect to find nestled in this snowy, mountain village. This piece coordinates with last year's accessory "Heidi & Her Goats" (set/4).

THE SOUND OF MUSIC® VON TRAPP VILLA (SET/5) . . . Bringing back fond memories of the classic musical and movie, *"The Sound Of Music®* von Trapp Villa" is the largest piece to date in *Alpine Village*. The grand three-story villa looks like a mansion and includes an entrance made of stone pillars with a wrought iron gate. The von Trapp family stands in front of their house rehearsing one of their favorite songs.

ALPINE VILLAGE ACCESSORIES . . . Villagers find that snowshoes and skis are essential for **"TREKKING IN THE SNOW"** (set/3), while **"ST. NICHOLAS"** stands proud, holding lots of presents in this year's *Alpine Village* accessories.

CHRISTMAS IN THE CITY

OLD TRINITY CHURCH . . . This astounding structure is a  must for collectors. The architecture of "Old Trinity Church" is Gothic; with its many peaks, tiers and buttresses adding another level of interest to this already spectacular church. The many windows are stained glass and add a hint of mystery and romance to the building.

PRECINCT 25 POLICE STATION . . . This city's fine police force deserves a top-notch headquarters and that's just what they receive with the new *"Precinct 25* Police Station." The building is festively decorated with a wreath on each of the first-floor windows and Christmas trees on the pillars of the second-story balcony. Spotlights shine in all directions, keeping a protective eye on the city.

THE UNIVERSITY CLUB . . . Friends come together for a little bit of "friendly competition" on the tennis court or in the indoor swimming pool at "The University Club." They can also catch up with one another in the restaurant or lounge.  Some, however, just like to relax at the spa and let the worries of Christmas shopping be forgotten.

THE WEDDING GALLERY . . . "The Wedding Gallery" is a one-stop shop for "couples-to-be." Customers in search of gorgeous wedding gowns and tuxedos can head downstairs, while those looking for invitations and honeymoon reservations only need to travel as far as the second floor. This  delightful boutique adds to the romantic nature of *Christmas in the City* and makes the perfect gift as a brass plate is available for engraving.

CHRISTMAS IN THE CITY ACCESSORIES . . . On her wedding day, **"A CARRIAGE RIDE FOR THE BRIDE"** will make her feel like she's Cinderella. Those who prefer the more modern comforts, however, can head to their reception in style in a black **"1919 FORD® MODEL-T."** Down the road, children get to meet the men hired **"TO PROTECT AND TO SERVE"** (set/3) and, while petting their horses, find out that mounted patrol is good, but it's the men in the **"CITY POLICE CAR"** that get to the scene the fastest. A man out for a joyride is **"READY FOR THE ROAD"** on his shiny new motorcycle.

Four new ornaments have been introduced into the *Christmas in the City* collection. **"CITY HALL"** and **"DOROTHY'S DRESS SHOP"** were available before, but were not lighted until now. Two first-time arrivals to the ornament selection are **"CATHEDRAL CHURCH OF ST. MARK"** and **"RED BRICK FIRE STATION."**

NORTH POLE

CUSTOM STITCHERS . . . This building (from the new *Elf Land* series) is where the elves' designer duds come from. Hanging outside are outfits that are ready to be sold, perhaps to draw in business. "Custom Stitchers" caters to small sizes only, as the sign out front points out. Bright lights inside offer the chance for a glimpse of next season's hottest fashion trends.

THE ELF SPA . . . Even the hard-working *Elf Land* residents need a little pampering and what better place to get it than "The Elf Spa." The spa is fully equipped with an outdoor jacuzzi for those looking to take a quick dip, while a sauna is available for those more interested in sweating off the days stress.

REAL PLASTIC SNOW FACTORY . . . Some may think it just falls from the sky, but don't be fooled. Village snow actually comes from the hard working elves at the "Real Plastic Snow Factory." The white stuff starts in the gold flaking tank on one side of the building, gets processed inside the factory and shows up in final form in the clear freezing tower on the other side. It then gets loaded into boxes, ready for a magical delivery.

REINDEER FLIGHT SCHOOL . . . If you've ever wondered how Santa's reindeer learn to fly, wonder no more! They take lessons at the "Reindeer Flight School," of course. The school is complete with a hangar and flight tower to lead the reindeer home (that is, if Rudolph isn't there to guide them). There's also a reindeer weather vane on the roof and bales of hay outside so tired reindeer can fuel up.

TILLIE'S TINY CUP CAFÉ . . . After a hard day's work residents of *Elf Land* head to the local café where they're sure to find good food and friends. "Tillie's Tiny Cup Café" allows the elves to thaw out with a hot bowl of soup and some hot chocolate. The quaint café is complete with windows that look like coffee cups and a bell on the front steps that Tillie rings when a fresh batch of cocoa is ready!

NORTH POLE ACCESSORIES . . . The first thing you see at the *North Pole* is the **"WELCOME TO ELF LAND"** entrance. If you listen carefully, you may even hear one of the three bells on the peaks ring as you pass through. You may also catch a glimpse of the elves **"LOADING THE SLEIGH"** or keeping in shape by having a **"CHRISTMAS FUN RUN"** (set/6). Many elves are getting ready for the holiday shopping season by **"DELIVERING REAL PLASTIC SNOW,"** while the reindeer prepare for the long flight at the **"REINDEER TRAINING CAMP"** (set/2). Several elves **"HAVE A SEAT"** (set/6) while taking a

well-deserved break during the busy day and more elves make a **"Dash Away Delivery."** Meanwhile, three **"Downhill Elves"** (set/2) have managed to sneak away for some winter fun.

There are four new ornaments in the *North Pole* this year. **"Santa's Lookout Tower"** is the only ornament that was re-introduced as a lighted ornament; the other three, **"Elf Bunkhouse," "Reindeer Barn"** and **"Santa's Workshop"** are new.

Two hinged boxes join the *North Pole* collection. **"Elf On A Sled"** is a brightly colored elf on his way down the hill and into your home, while the **"Caroling Elf"** has an open songbook in hand and is ready to sing his heart out just for you!

General Heritage Village

***General Heritage Village Accessories* . . .** The **"Painting Our Own Village Sign"** accessory is a great way to bring some advertising to the village, while several other new accessories add motion to your collection, including the new animated **"Ski Slope"** and the **"Up, Up & Away Witch."** For villagers looking to travel, the new **"Biplane Up In The Sky"** is the fastest method, but the **"Village Express Electric Train Set"** (set/24) is a viable alternative for more down-to-earth village travelers.

E ach year Department 56 announces the Heritage Village retirements in *USA Today,* as well as on their web site (*www.department56.com*). This year a new feature of the web site was introduced. Collectors interested in their own copy of the announcement were allowed to pre-register to receive an e-mail from the company on the morning of the retirements. The following Heritage Village pieces (listed with issue year in parentheses) were retired on November 6, 1998.

DICKENS' VILLAGE
- ❑ Blenham Street Bank (1995)
- ❑ Boarding & Lodging School (1994)
- ❑ Canadian Trading Co.(1997)
- ❑ Dickens' Village Start A Tradition Set (1997, set/13)
- ❑ J.D. Nichols Toy Shop (1995)
- ❑ Kensington Palace (1998, set/23)
- ❑ King's Road Post Office (1992)
- ❑ The Maltings (1995)
- ❑ The Old Globe Theatre (LE-1998, set/4, *Historical Landmark Series*)
- ❑ Seton Morris Spice Merchant (1998, set/10)
- ❑ T. Puddlewick Spectacle Shop (1995)
- ❑ Victoria Station (1989)
- ❑ Whittlesbourne Church (1994)

NEW ENGLAND VILLAGE
- ❑ Cape Keag Fish Cannery (1994)
- ❑ Chowder House (1995)
- ❑ J. Hudson Stoveworks (1996)
- ❑ Old North Church (1988)
- ❑ Pigeonhead Lighthouse (1994)
- ❑ Woodbridge Post Office (1995)

ALPINE VILLAGE
- ❑ Bakery & Chocolate Shop (1994)
- ❑ Kukuck Uhren (1992)
- ❑ Sport Laden (1993)

CHRISTMAS IN THE CITY
- ❑ All Saints Corner Church (1991)
- ❑ Brighton School (1995)
- ❑ The Capitol (1997)
- ❑ Heritage Museum Of Art (1994)
- ❑ Pickford Place (1995)
- ❑ Scottie's Toy Shop (1998, set/10)
- ❑ Washington Street Post Office (1996)

NORTH POLE
- ❑ Elfin Forge & Assembly Shop (1995)
- ❑ Elsie's Gingerbread (LE-1998)
- ❑ Elves' Trade School (1995)
- ❑ North Pole Express Depot (1993)
- ❑ Santa's Bell Repair (1996)

GENERAL HERITAGE VILLAGE ACCESSORIES
❑ Village Streetcar (1994, set/10)
❑ Village Animated Ski Mountain (1996)

DICKENS' VILLAGE ACCESSORIES
❑ Bringing Fleeces To The Mill (1993, set/2)
❑ Bringing Home The Yule Log (1991, set/3)
❑ Chelsea Market Curiosities Monger & Cart (1994, set/2)
❑ Chelsea Market Mistletoe Monger & Cart (1994, set/2)
❑ The Flying Scot Train (1990, set/4)
❑ Holiday Coach (1991)
❑ King's Road Cab (1989)
❑ Portobello Road Peddlers (1994, set/3)
❑ "Tallyho!" (1995, set/5)

NEW ENGLAND VILLAGE ACCESSORIES
❑ Lumberjacks (1995, set/2)
❑ A New Potbellied Stove For Christmas (1996, set/2)
❑ The Old Man And The Sea (1994, set/3)
❑ Over The River And Through The Woods (1994)

ALPINE VILLAGE ACCESSORIES
❑ The Toy Peddler (1990, set/3)

CHRISTMAS IN THE CITY ACCESSORIES
❑ Caroling Thru The City (1991, set/3)
❑ Chamber Orchestra (1994, set/4)

CHRISTMAS IN THE CITY ACCESSORIES, CONT.
❑ Choirboys All-In-A-Row (1995)
❑ Holiday Field Trip (1994, set/3)
❑ Mailbox & Fire Hydrant (1990, set/2)
❑ One-Man Band And The Dancing Dog (1995, set/2)

NORTH POLE ACCESSORIES
❑ I'll Need More Toys (1995, set/2)
❑ Last Minute Delivery (1994)
❑ North Pole Gate (1993)
❑ Sing A Song For Santa (1993, set/3)

DICKENS' VILLAGE ORNAMENTS
❑ Dickens' Village Church (1997, *Classic Ornament Series*)
❑ Dickens' Village Mill (1997, *Classic Ornament Series*)
❑ Old Curiosity Shop (1997, *Classic Ornament Series*)

NEW ENGLAND VILLAGE ORNAMENTS
❑ Craggy Cove Lighthouse (1997, *Classic Ornament Series*)

CHRISTMAS IN THE CITY ORNAMENTS
❑ City Hall (1997, *Classic Ornament Series*)
❑ Dorothy's Dress Shop (1997, *Classic Ornament Series*)

NORTH POLE ORNAMENTS
❑ North Pole Santa's Workshop (1997, *Classic Ornament Series*)
❑ Santa's Lookout Tower (1997, *Classic Ornament Series*)

HERITAGE VILLAGE TOP TEN

*T*his section highlights the ten most valuable pieces in Heritage Village as determined by their value on the secondary market. Our market meter shows the percentage increase of each piece from its issue price.

DICKENS' VILLAGE MILL (LE-2,500)
Dickens' Village, #6519-6
Issued 1985 • Retired 1986
Issue Price: $35 • Market Value: **$5,000**
Market Meter: +14,186%

Collectors didn't know it at the time, but this mill was the first limited edition of *Dickens' Village.* Its production run of only 2,500 pieces made it a hard piece to acquire when it was current and, now that it's retired, it's a great deal more difficult to find.

NORMAN CHURCH (LE-3,500)
Dickens' Village, #6502-1
Issued 1986 • Retired 1987
Issue Price: $40 • Market Value: **$3,340**
Market Meter: +8,250%

The "Norman Church" was the second limited edition of *Dickens' Village* and, subsequently, ranks as the second most valuable piece in the collection. Only 3,500 pieces were produced before the building was retired a year after first being released.

CATHEDRAL CHURCH OF ST. MARK (LE-3,024)
Christmas in the City, #5549-2
Issued 1991 • Retired 1993
Issue Price: $120 • Market Value: **$2,100**
Market Meter: +1,650%

A variety of production problems such as cracks and breaks led to the early retirement of this piece. Of the 17,500 pieces planned for this limited edition, only 3,024 were actually produced. The number of pieces available to collectors, however, is substantially less as many broken pieces were returned by retailers.

CHESTERTON MANOR HOUSE (LE-7,500)
Dickens' Village, #6568-4
Issued 1987 • Retired 1988
Issue Price: $45 • Market Value: **$1,540**
Market Meter: +3,323%

"Chesterton Manor House" retired just one year after its release in 1987. Problems such as firing cracks and a fragile chimney make this limited edition building of 7,500 hard to find in mint condition.

THE ORIGINAL SHOPS OF DICKENS' VILLAGE (SET/7)
Dickens' Village, #6515-3
Issued 1984 • Retired 1988
Issue Price: $175 • Market Value: **$1,325**
Market Meter: +658%

"The Original Shops Of Dickens' Village" was the first release of *Dickens' Village*. Many retailers allowed this set to be broken and sold individually, which makes a complete set a rare find on the secondary market.

NEW ENGLAND VILLAGE (SET/7)
New England Village, #6530-7
Issued 1986 • Retired 1989
Issue Price: $170 • Market Value: **$1,220**
Market Meter: +618%

This set of seven buildings pioneered the *New England Village* collection in 1987. Like the previous *Dickens' Village* set, many pieces were separated for individual sale.

SMYTHE WOOLEN MILL (LE-7,500)
New England Village, #6543-9
Issued 1987 • Retired 1988
Issue Price: $42 • Market Value: **$1,100**
Market Meter: +2,520%

"Smythe Woolen Mill" is the only limited edition building in *New England Village* and was coveted by collectors of both *New England Village* and *Dickens' Village*.

JOSEF ENGEL FARMHOUSE
Alpine Village, #5952-8
Issued 1987 • Retired 1989
Issue Price: $33 • Market Value: $1,030
Market Meter: +3,022%

"Josef Engel Farmhouse" has the distinction of being the first building to retire from *Alpine Village*. Available only for two years, this piece is difficult to find in mint condition due to corners that frequently chipped and stairs that, through the years, became unglued.

DICKENS' COTTAGES (SET/3)
Dickens' Village, #6518-8
Issued 1985 • Retired 1988
Issue Price: $75 • Market Value: $1,000
Market Meter: +1,234%

Introduced in 1985, the three cottages in this set were nameless for two years. One of them, "Stone Cottage," comes in green or tan, with the tan version being worth slightly more on the secondary market.

PALACE THEATRE
Christmas in the City, #5963-3
Issued 1987 • Retired 1989
Issue Price: $45 • Market Value: $955
Market Meter: +2,023%

This *Christmas in the City* piece gained popularity on the secondary market due to the spread of a rumor. The "Palace Theatre" was available for two years, but talk of a shipment

never arriving to retailers caused collectors to turn to the secondary market in order to find the piece. From the beginning, the "Palace Theatre" was known to break or suffer from faults in the walls.

How To Use Your Collector's Value Guide™

Ashbury Inn
Issued: 1991 • Retired: 1995
#5555-7 • Original Price: $55
Market Value: $78

1. LOCATE your piece within the Value Guide. The Heritage Village Collection is grouped according to village in the following order: *Dickens' Village, New England Village, Alpine Village, Christmas in the City, North Pole, Disney Parks Village Series* and *Little Town of Bethlehem.* All village buildings are listed first and are immediately followed by accessories. Within each section, all pieces are listed alphabetically. Buildings that are part of a set are shown individually following the set. For example, "Stone Cottage" can be found right after its set, "Dickens' Cottages." Helpful indexes can be found in the back of the book to help you locate your pieces.

2. FIND the market value of your piece. Market values for variations are listed in parentheses following the original piece's value. Pieces for which secondary market pricing is not established are listed as "N/E" and all available pieces are listed with their current retail price.

3. RECORD in pencil the year of purchase, price paid and current value in the corresponding boxes at the bottom of each Value Guide page.

DICKENS' VILLAGE – BUILDINGS –		
Year Purchased	Price Paid	Value Of My Collection
1. 5/21/92	55.00	78.00
2.		
3.		
3a.		
3b.		
PENCIL TOTALS		

4. CALCULATE the total value for each page by adding all of the boxes in each column.

5. TRANSFER the totals from each page to the "Total Value Of My Collection" worksheets beginning on page 117.

6. ADD the page totals together to determine the value of your collection!

DICKENS' VILLAGE BUILDINGS

Dickens' Village is the oldest village in the Heritage Village Collection. Out of the 123 buildings which have been introduced since 1984, 93 have since been retired. Of these, the "Dickens' Village Mill," a limited edition of only 2,500 pieces, is currently the most valuable piece on the secondary market.

Ashbury Inn
Issued: 1991 • Retired: 1995
#5555-7 • Original Price: $55
Market Value: $78

Ashwick Lane Hose & Ladder
Issued: 1997 • Current
#58305 • Original Price: $54
Market Value: $54

Barley Bree (set/2)
Issued: 1987 • Retired: 1989
#5900-5 • Original Price: $60
Market Value: $395

Barn
Issued: 1987 • Retired: 1989
#5900-5 • Original Price: $30
Market Value: N/E

Farmhouse
Issued: 1987 • Retired: 1989
#5900-5 • Original Price: $30
Market Value: N/E

DICKENS' VILLAGE
– BUILDINGS –

	Year Purchased	Price Paid	Value Of My Collection
1.			
2.			
3.			
3a.			
3b.			
PENCIL TOTALS			

29

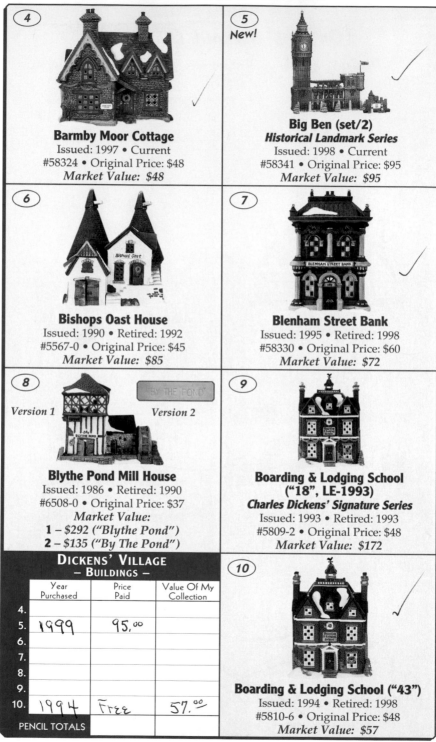

4

Barmby Moor Cottage
Issued: 1997 • Current
#58324 • Original Price: $48
Market Value: $48

5

New!

Big Ben (set/2)
Historical Landmark Series
Issued: 1998 • Current
#58341 • Original Price: $95
Market Value: $95

6

Bishops Oast House
Issued: 1990 • Retired: 1992
#5567-0 • Original Price: $45
Market Value: $85

7

Blenham Street Bank
Issued: 1995 • Retired: 1998
#58330 • Original Price: $60
Market Value: $72

8

Version 1   *Version 2*

Blythe Pond Mill House
Issued: 1986 • Retired: 1990
#6508-0 • Original Price: $37
Market Value:
1 – *$292 ("Blythe Pond")*
2 – *$135 ("By The Pond")*

9

**Boarding & Lodging School
("18", LE-1993)**
Charles Dickens' Signature Series
Issued: 1993 • Retired: 1993
#5809-2 • Original Price: $48
Market Value: $172

DICKENS' VILLAGE
– BUILDINGS –

	Year Purchased	Price Paid	Value Of My Collection
4.			
5.	1999	95.⁰⁰	
6.			
7.			
8.			
9.			
10.	1994	Free	57.⁰⁰
PENCIL TOTALS			

10

Boarding & Lodging School ("43")
Issued: 1994 • Retired: 1998
#5810-6 • Original Price: $48
Market Value: $57

11

Brick Abbey
Issued: 1987 • Retired: 1989
#6549-8 • Original Price: $33
Market Value: $375

12

Butter Tub Barn
Issued: 1996 • Current
#58338 • Original Price: $48
Market Value: $48

13

Butter Tub Farmhouse
Issued: 1996 • Current
#58337 • Original Price: $40
Market Value: $40

14

C. Fletcher Public House (LE-12,500)
Issued: 1988 • Retired: 1989
#5904-8 • Original Price: $35
Market Value: $555

15

Chadbury Station And Train
Issued: 1986 • Retired: 1989
#6528-5 • Original Price: $65
Market Value: $405

16

Chesterton Manor House (LE-7,500)
Issued: 1987 • Retired: 1988
#6568-4 • Original Price: $45
Market Value: $1,540

17

Christmas Carol Cottage
(with magic smoking element)
Christmas Carol Revisited
Issued: 1996 • Current
#58339 • Original Price: $60
Market Value: $60

DICKENS' VILLAGE
– BUILDINGS –

	Year Purchased	Price Paid	Value Of My Collection
11.			
12.			
13.			
14.			
15.			
16.			
17.			
PENCIL TOTALS			

DICKENS' VILLAGE
– BUILDINGS –

(18)

Christmas Carol Cottages (set/3)
Issued: 1986 • Retired: 1995
#6500-5 • Original Price: $75
Market Value: $140

(18a)

The Cottage Of Bob Cratchit & Tiny Tim
Issued: 1986 • Retired: 1995
#6500-5 • Original Price: $25
Market Value: $68

(18b)

Fezziwig's Warehouse
Issued: 1986 • Retired: 1995
#6500-5 • Original Price: $25
Market Value: $45

(18c)

Scrooge & Marley Counting House
Issued: 1986 • Retired: 1995
#6500-5 • Original Price: $25
Market Value: $54

(19)

Cobblestone Shops (set/3)
Issued: 1988 • Retired: 1990
#5924-2 • Original Price: $95
Market Value: $375

(19a)

Booter And Cobbler
Issued: 1988 • Retired: 1990
#5924-2 • Original Price: $32
Market Value: $130

DICKENS' VILLAGE
– BUILDINGS –

	Year Purchased	Price Paid	Value Of My Collection
18.			
18a.			
18b.			
18c.			
19.			
19a.			
19b.			
PENCIL TOTALS			

(19b)

T. Wells Fruit & Spice Shop
Issued: 1988 • Retired: 1990
#5924-2 • Original Price: $32
Market Value: $100

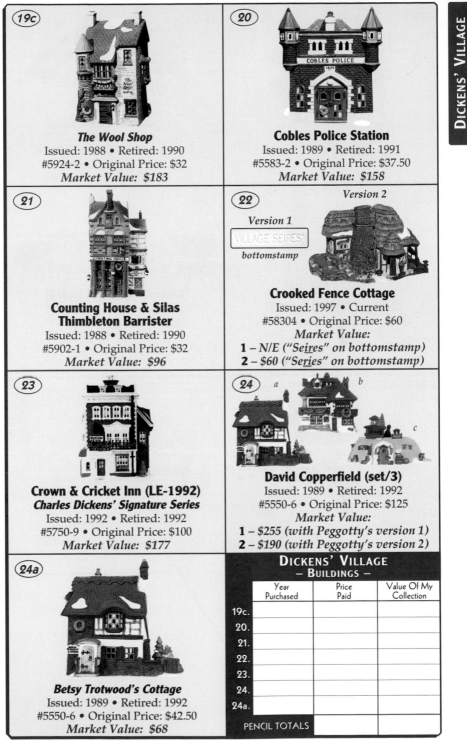

19c

The Wool Shop
Issued: 1988 • Retired: 1990
#5924-2 • Original Price: $32
Market Value: $183

20

Cobles Police Station
Issued: 1989 • Retired: 1991
#5583-2 • Original Price: $37.50
Market Value: $158

21

Counting House & Silas Thimbleton Barrister
Issued: 1988 • Retired: 1990
#5902-1 • Original Price: $32
Market Value: $96

22

Version 1

bottomstamp

Version 2

Crooked Fence Cottage
Issued: 1997 • Current
#58304 • Original Price: $60
Market Value:
1 – N/E ("Seires" on bottomstamp)
2 – $60 ("Series" on bottomstamp)

23

Crown & Cricket Inn (LE-1992)
Charles Dickens' Signature Series
Issued: 1992 • Retired: 1992
#5750-9 • Original Price: $100
Market Value: $177

24
a   b   c

David Copperfield (set/3)
Issued: 1989 • Retired: 1992
#5550-6 • Original Price: $125
Market Value:
1 – $255 (with Peggotty's version 1)
2 – $190 (with Peggotty's version 2)

24a

Betsy Trotwood's Cottage
Issued: 1989 • Retired: 1992
#5550-6 • Original Price: $42.50
Market Value: $68

DICKENS' VILLAGE
– BUILDINGS –

	Year Purchased	Price Paid	Value Of My Collection
19c.			
20.			
21.			
22.			
23.			
24.			
24a.			
PENCIL TOTALS			

(24b)

Mr. Wickfield Solicitor
Issued: 1989 • Retired: 1992
#5550-6 • Original Price: $42.50
Market Value: $102

(24c) *Version 1*   *Version 2*

Peggotty's Seaside Cottage
Issued: 1989 • Retired: 1992
#5550-6 • Original Price: $42.50
Market Value:
1 – $140 (tan) 2 – $72 (green)

(25)

Dedlock Arms (LE-1994)
Charles Dickens' Signature Series
Issued: 1994 • Retired: 1994
#5752-5 • Original Price: $100
Market Value: $142

(26) *a   b   c*

Dickens' Cottages (set/3)
Issued: 1985 • Retired: 1988
#6518-8 • Original Price: $75
Market Value:
1 – $1,000 (with Stone Cottage version 1)
2 – $920 (with Stone Cottage version 2)

(26a) *Version 1*   *Version 2*

Stone Cottage
Issued: 1985 • Retired: 1988
#6518-8 • Original Price: $25
Market Value: 1 – $470 (tan) 2 – $390 (green)

Dickens' Village
– Buildings –

	Year Purchased	Price Paid	Value Of My Collection
24b.			
24c.			
25.			
26.			
26a.			
PENCIL TOTALS			

(26b)

Thatched Cottage
Issued: 1985 • Retired: 1988
#6518-8 • Original Price: $25
Market Value: $200

(26c)

Tudor Cottage
Issued: 1985 • Retired: 1988
#6518-8 • Original Price: $25
Market Value: $400

(27)

Dickens' Lane Shops (set/3)
Issued: 1986 • Retired: 1989
#6507-2 • Original Price: $80
Market Value: $600

(27a)

Cottage Toy Shop
Issued: 1986 • Retired: 1989
#6507-2 • Original Price: $27
Market Value: $225

(27b)

Thomas Kersey Coffee House
Issued: 1986 • Retired: 1989
#6507-2 • Original Price: $27
Market Value: $180

(27c)

Tuttle's Pub
Issued: 1986 • Retired: 1989
#6507-2 • Original Price: $27
Market Value: $232

DICKENS' VILLAGE
– BUILDINGS –

	Year Purchased	Price Paid	Value Of My Collection
26b.			
26c.			
27.			
27a.			
27b.			
27c.			
PENCIL TOTALS			

DICKENS' VILLAGE
– BUILDINGS –

35

28

Version 1 — Version 2 — Version 3 — Version 4 — Version 5

Dickens' Village Church
Issued: 1985 • Retired: 1989
#6516-1 • Original Price: $35
Market Value: **1** – *$420 (white)* **2** – *$285 (cream)* **3** – *$350 (green)*
4 – *$190 (tan)* **5** – *$170 (butterscotch)*

29

Dickens' Village Mill (LE-2,500)
Issued: 1985 • Retired: 1986
#6519-6 • Original Price: $35
Market Value: $5,000

30

Old East Rectory — Sudbury Church

The Spirit Of Giving

Dickens' Village Start A Tradition Set
(set/13, Event Piece)
Issued: 1997 • Retired: 1998
#58322 • Original Price: $75
Market Value: $105

31

Dudden Cross Church
Issued: 1995 • Retired: 1997
#5834-3 • Original Price: $45
Market Value: $52

32

Dursley Manor
Issued: 1995 • Current
#58329 • Original Price: $50
Market Value: $55

DICKENS' VILLAGE
– BUILDINGS –

	Year Purchased	Price Paid	Value Of My Collection
28.			
29.			
30.			
31.			
32.			
33.			
PENCIL TOTALS			

33

East Indies Trading Co.
Issued: 1997 • Current
#58302 • Original Price: $65
Market Value: $65

(34)

Fagin's Hide-A-Way
Issued: 1991 • Retired: 1995
#5552-2 • Original Price: $68
Market Value: $92

(35)

Version 1   Version 2

The Flat Of Ebenezer Scrooge
Issued: 1989 • Current
#5587-5 • Original Price: $37.50
Market Value: 1 – $37.50 (with panes)
2 – N/E (without panes)

(36)

Gad's Hill Place (LE-1997)
Charles Dickens' Signature Series
Issued: 1997 • Retired: 1997
#57535 • Original Price: $98
Market Value: $126

(37)

Giggelswick Mutton & Ham
Issued: 1994 • Retired: 1997
#5822-0 • Original Price: $48
Market Value: $60

(38)

The Grapes Inn (LE-1996)
Charles Dickens' Signature Series
Issued: 1996 • Retired: 1996
#57534 • Original Price: $120
Market Value: $145

(39)

Great Denton Mill
Issued: 1993 • Retired: 1997
#5812-2 • Original Price: $50
Market Value: $60

(40)
New!

Great Expectations Satis Manor
(set/4, with book)
Literary Classics
Issued: 1998 • Current
#58310 • Original Price: $110
Market Value: $110

DICKENS' VILLAGE
– BUILDINGS –

	Year Purchased	Price Paid	Value Of My Collection
34.			
35.			
36.			
37.			
38.			
39.			
40.			
PENCIL TOTALS			

DICKENS' VILLAGE – BUILDINGS –

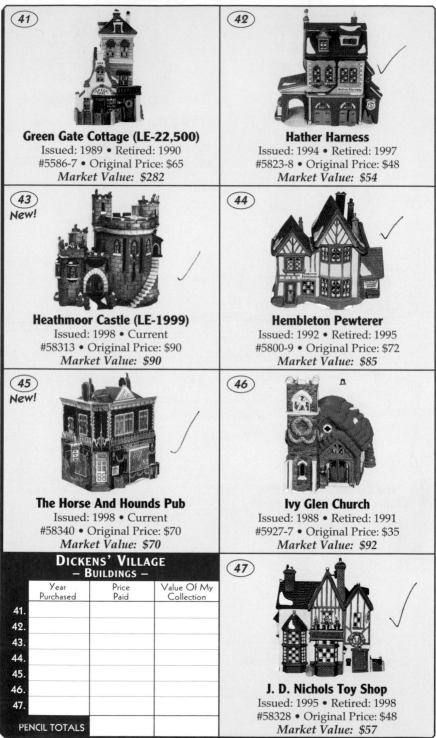

41

Green Gate Cottage (LE-22,500)
Issued: 1989 • Retired: 1990
#5586-7 • Original Price: $65
Market Value: $282

42

Hather Harness
Issued: 1994 • Retired: 1997
#5823-8 • Original Price: $48
Market Value: $54

43 New!

Heathmoor Castle (LE-1999)
Issued: 1998 • Current
#58313 • Original Price: $90
Market Value: $90

44

Hembleton Pewterer
Issued: 1992 • Retired: 1995
#5800-9 • Original Price: $72
Market Value: $85

45 New!

The Horse And Hounds Pub
Issued: 1998 • Current
#58340 • Original Price: $70
Market Value: $70

46

Ivy Glen Church
Issued: 1988 • Retired: 1991
#5927-7 • Original Price: $35
Market Value: $92

DICKENS' VILLAGE
– BUILDINGS –

	Year Purchased	Price Paid	Value Of My Collection
41.			
42.			
43.			
44.			
45.			
46.			
47.			
PENCIL TOTALS			

47

J. D. Nichols Toy Shop
Issued: 1995 • Retired: 1998
#58328 • Original Price: $48
Market Value: $57

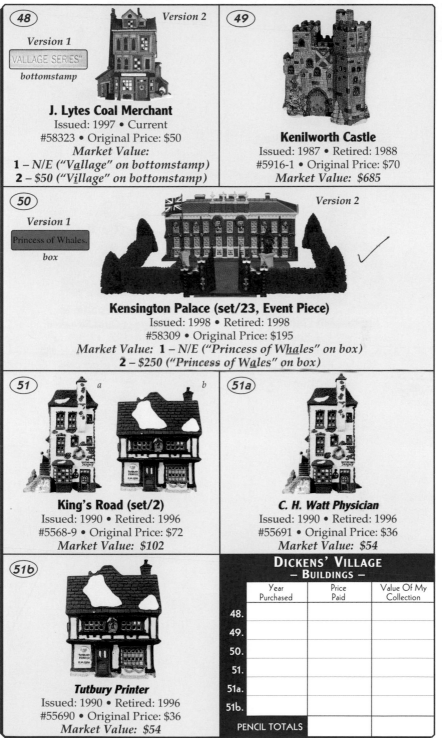

48

Version 1

VALLAGE SERIES"
bottomstamp

Version 2

J. Lytes Coal Merchant
Issued: 1997 • Current
#58323 • Original Price: $50
Market Value:
1 – *N/E ("Vallage" on bottomstamp)*
2 – *$50 ("Village" on bottomstamp)*

49

Kenilworth Castle
Issued: 1987 • Retired: 1988
#5916-1 • Original Price: $70
Market Value: $685

50

Version 1

Princess of Whales,
box

Version 2

Kensington Palace (set/23, Event Piece)
Issued: 1998 • Retired: 1998
#58309 • Original Price: $195
Market Value: **1** – *N/E ("Princess of Whales" on box)*
2 – *$250 ("Princess of Wales" on box)*

51   a   b

King's Road (set/2)
Issued: 1990 • Retired: 1996
#5568-9 • Original Price: $72
Market Value: $102

51a

C. H. Watt Physician
Issued: 1990 • Retired: 1996
#55691 • Original Price: $36
Market Value: $54

51b

Tutbury Printer
Issued: 1990 • Retired: 1996
#55690 • Original Price: $36
Market Value: $54

DICKENS' VILLAGE
– BUILDINGS –

	Year Purchased	Price Paid	Value Of My Collection
48.			
49.			
50.			
51.			
51a.			
51b.			
PENCIL TOTALS			

52

King's Road Post Office
Issued: 1992 • Retired: 1998
#5801-7 • Original Price: $45
Market Value: $52

53

Kingsford's Brew House
Issued: 1993 • Retired: 1996
#5811-4 • Original Price: $45
Market Value: $62

54

Knottinghill Church
Issued: 1989 • Retired: 1995
#5582-4 • Original Price: $50
Market Value: $73

55

Leacock Poulterer
Christmas Carol Revisited
Issued: 1997 • Current
#58303 • Original Price: $48
Market Value: $48

56
New!

Lynton Point Tower
Issued: 1998 • Current
#58315 • Original Price: $80
Market Value: $80

57

The Maltings
Issued: 1995 • Retired: 1998
#5833-5 • Original Price: $50
Market Value: $55

DICKENS' VILLAGE
– BUILDINGS –

	Year Purchased	Price Paid	Value Of My Collection
52.			
53.			
54.			
55.			
56.			
57.			
PENCIL TOTALS			

58

Frogmore Chemist | G. Choir's Weights & Scales | Lydby Trunk & Satchel Shop | Custom House

Manchester Square (set/25)
Issued: 1997 • Current
#58301 • Original Price: $250
Market Value: $250

Manchester Square Accessory

59

The Melancholy Tavern
Christmas Carol Revisited
Issued: 1996 • Current
#58347 • Original Price: $45
Market Value: $45

60

a | b | c | d | e

Merchant Shops (set/5)
Issued: 1988 • Retired: 1993
#5926-9 • Original Price: $150
Market Value: $265

60a

Geo. Weeton Watchmaker
Issued: 1988 • Retired: 1993
#5926-9 • Original Price: $32.50
Market Value: $57

60b

The Mermaid Fish Shoppe
Issued: 1988 • Retired: 1993
#5926-9 • Original Price: $32.50
Market Value: $78

60c

Poulterer
Issued: 1988 • Retired: 1993
#5926-9 • Original Price: $32.50
Market Value: $62

DICKENS' VILLAGE
– BUILDINGS –

	Year Purchased	Price Paid	Value Of My Collection
58.			
59.			
60.			
60a.			
60b.			
60c.			
PENCIL TOTALS			

DICKENS' VILLAGE – BUILDINGS –

60d

Walpole Tailors
Issued: 1988 • Retired: 1993
#5926-9 • Original Price: $32.50
Market Value: $57

60e

White Horse Bakery
Issued: 1988 • Retired: 1993
#5926-9 • Original Price: $32.50
Market Value: $65

61

Mulberrie Court
Issued: 1996 • Current
#58345 • Original Price: $90
Market Value: $90

62

Nephew Fred's Flat
Issued: 1991 • Retired: 1994
#5557-3 • Original Price: $35
Market Value: $82

63

Nettie Quinn Puppets & Marionettes
Issued: 1996 • Current
#58344 • Original Price: $50
Market Value: $50

64

a   b

Nicholas Nickleby (set/2)
Issued: 1988 • Retired: 1991
#5925-0 • Original Price: $72
Market Value:
1 – *$195 (with Nickleby Cottage version 1)*
2 – *$172 (with Nickleby Cottage version 2)*

DICKENS' VILLAGE
– BUILDINGS –

	Year Purchased	Price Paid	Value Of My Collection
60d.			
60e.			
61.			
62.			
63.			
64.			
PENCIL TOTALS			

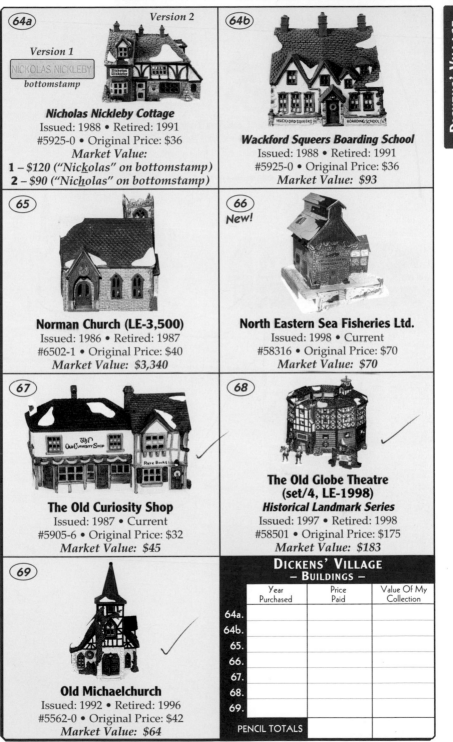

(64a)

Version 1

NICKOLAS NICKLEBY
bottomstamp

Version 2

Nicholas Nickleby Cottage
Issued: 1988 • Retired: 1991
#5925-0 • Original Price: $36
Market Value:
1 – $120 *("Nickolas" on bottomstamp)*
2 – $90 *("Nicholas" on bottomstamp)*

(64b)

WACKFORD SQUEERS   BOARDING SCHOOL

Wackford Squeers Boarding School
Issued: 1988 • Retired: 1991
#5925-0 • Original Price: $36
Market Value: $93

(65)

Norman Church (LE-3,500)
Issued: 1986 • Retired: 1987
#6502-1 • Original Price: $40
Market Value: $3,340

(66)
New!

North Eastern Sea Fisheries Ltd.
Issued: 1998 • Current
#58316 • Original Price: $70
Market Value: $70

(67)

The Old Curiosity Shop
Rare Books

The Old Curiosity Shop
Issued: 1987 • Current
#5905-6 • Original Price: $32
Market Value: $45

(68)

The Old Globe Theatre
(set/4, LE-1998)
Historical Landmark Series
Issued: 1997 • Retired: 1998
#58501 • Original Price: $175
Market Value: $183

(69)

Old Michaelchurch
Issued: 1992 • Retired: 1996
#5562-0 • Original Price: $42
Market Value: $64

DICKENS' VILLAGE
– BUILDINGS –

	Year Purchased	Price Paid	Value Of My Collection
64a.			
64b.			
65.			
66.			
67.			
68.			
69.			
PENCIL TOTALS			

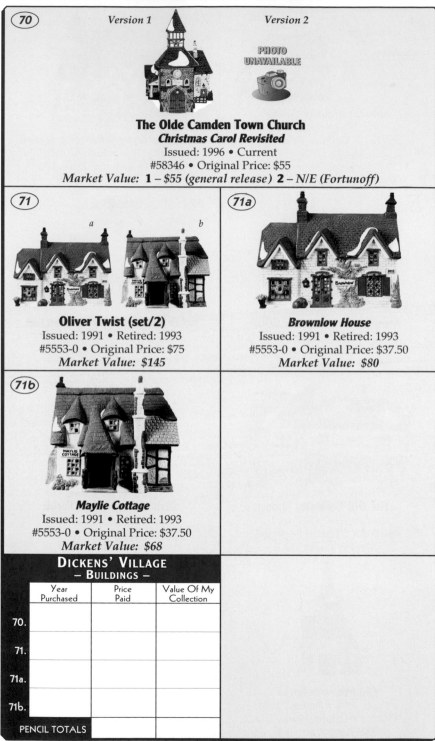

70

Version 1   Version 2

PHOTO UNAVAILABLE

The Olde Camden Town Church
Christmas Carol Revisited
Issued: 1996 • Current
#58346 • Original Price: $55
Market Value: **1** – $55 *(general release)* **2** – N/E *(Fortunoff)*

71

a   b

Oliver Twist (set/2)
Issued: 1991 • Retired: 1993
#5553-0 • Original Price: $75
Market Value: $145

71a

Brownlow House
Issued: 1991 • Retired: 1993
#5553-0 • Original Price: $37.50
Market Value: $80

71b

Maylie Cottage
Issued: 1991 • Retired: 1993
#5553-0 • Original Price: $37.50
Market Value: $68

DICKENS' VILLAGE
– BUILDINGS –

	Year Purchased	Price Paid	Value Of My Collection
70.			
71.			
71a.			
71b.			
PENCIL TOTALS			

72

The Original Shops Of Dickens' Village (set/7)
Issued: 1984 • Retired: 1988
#6515-3 • Original Price: $175
Market Value: $1,325

72a

Abel Beesley Butcher
Issued: 1984 • Retired: 1988
#6515-3 • Original Price: $25
Market Value: $134

72b

Bean And Son Smithy Shop
Issued: 1984 • Retired: 1988
#6515-3 • Original Price: $25
Market Value: $200

72c

Candle Shop
Issued: 1984 • Retired: 1988
#6515-3 • Original Price: $25
Market Value: $200

72d

Crowntree Inn
Issued: 1984 • Retired: 1988
#6515-3 • Original Price: $25
Market Value: $305

72e

Golden Swan Baker
Issued: 1984 • Retired: 1988
#6515-3 • Original Price: $25
Market Value: $190

DICKENS' VILLAGE – Buildings –		
Year Purchased	Price Paid	Value Of My Collection
72.		
72a.		
72b.		
72c.		
72d.		
72e.		
PENCIL TOTALS		

(72f)

Green Grocer
Issued: 1984 • Retired: 1988
#6515-3 • Original Price: $25
Market Value: $200

(72g)

Jones & Co. Brush & Basket Shop
Issued: 1984 • Retired: 1988
#6515-3 • Original Price: $25
Market Value: $298

(73)

The Pied Bull Inn (LE-1993)
Charles Dickens' Signature Series
Issued: 1993 • Retired: 1993
#5751-7 • Original Price: $100
Market Value: $160

(74)

**Portobello Road Thatched
Cottages (set/3)**
Issued: 1994 • Retired: 1997
#5824-6 • Original Price: $120
Market Value: $130

(74a)

Browning Cottage
Issued: 1994 • Retired: 1997
#58249 • Original Price: $40
Market Value: $45

DICKENS' VILLAGE
– BUILDINGS –

	Year Purchased	Price Paid	Value Of My Collection
72f.			
72g.			
73.			
74.			
74a.			
PENCIL TOTALS			

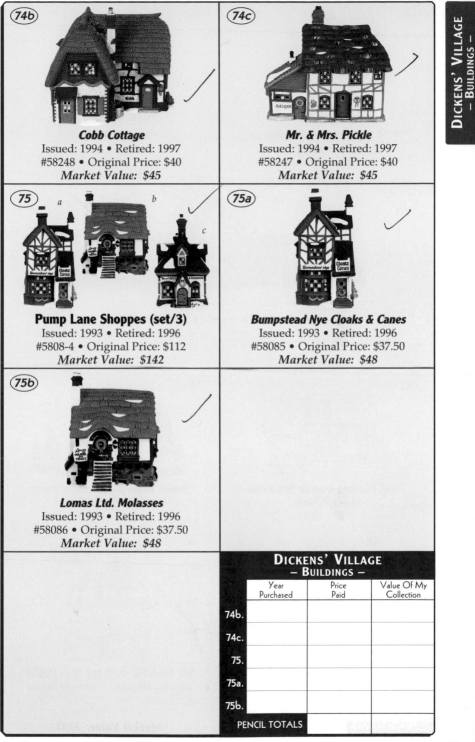

(74b)

Cobb Cottage
Issued: 1994 • Retired: 1997
#58248 • Original Price: $40
Market Value: $45

(74c)

Mr. & Mrs. Pickle
Issued: 1994 • Retired: 1997
#58247 • Original Price: $40
Market Value: $45

(75)

Pump Lane Shoppes (set/3)
Issued: 1993 • Retired: 1996
#5808-4 • Original Price: $112
Market Value: $142

(75a)

Bumpstead Nye Cloaks & Canes
Issued: 1993 • Retired: 1996
#58085 • Original Price: $37.50
Market Value: $48

(75b)

Lomas Ltd. Molasses
Issued: 1993 • Retired: 1996
#58086 • Original Price: $37.50
Market Value: $48

DICKENS' VILLAGE
– BUILDINGS –

	Year Purchased	Price Paid	Value Of My Collection
74b.			
74c.			
75.			
75a.			
75b.			
PENCIL TOTALS			

DICKENS' VILLAGE – BUILDINGS –

75c

W.M. Wheat Cakes & Puddings
Issued: 1993 • Retired: 1996
#58087 • Original Price: $37.50
Market Value: $48

76

Quilly's Antiques
Issued: 1996 • Current
#58348 • Original Price: $46
Market Value: $46

77

Ramsford Palace

Corner Wall Topiaries

Wall Hedge

Palace Fountain   Palace Gate   Palace Guards
Ramsford Palace (set/17, LE-27,500)
Issued: 1996 • Retired: 1996
#58336 • Original Price: $175
Market Value: $550

78

**Ruth Marion Scotch Woolens
(LE-17,500)**
Issued: 1989 • Retired: 1990
#5585-9 • Original Price: $65
Market Value: $390

79

Seton Morris
Spice Merchant

Christmas
Apples

**Seton Morris Spice Merchant
(set/10, Event Piece)**
Issued: 1998 • Retired: 1998
#58308 • Original Price: $65
Market Value: $75

**DICKENS' VILLAGE
– BUILDINGS –**

	Year Purchased	Price Paid	Value Of My Collection
75c.			
76.			
77.			
78.			
79.			
80.			
PENCIL TOTALS			

80

Sir John Falstaff Inn (LE-1995)
Charles Dickens' Signature Series
Issued: 1995 • Retired: 1995
#5753-3 • Original Price: $100
Market Value: $135

DICKENS' VILLAGE — BUILDINGS —

81

Faversham Lamps & Oil

Town Square Carolers

Morston Steak & Kidney Pie

Town Square Shops (set/2)

Start A Tradition Set (set/13)
Issued: 1995 • Retired: 1996
#5832-7 • Original Price: $85
Market Value: $110

82 New!

Tattyeave Knoll
Issued: 1998 • Current
#58311 • Original Price: $55
Market Value: $55

83 New!

Teaman & Crupp China Shop
Issued: 1998 • Current
#58314 • Original Price: $64
Market Value: $64

84

Theatre Royal
Issued: 1989 • Retired: 1992
#5584-0 • Original Price: $45
Market Value: $90

85

Thomas Mudge Timepieces
Issued: 1998 • Current
#58307 • Original Price: $60
Market Value: $60

86

Tower Of London (set/5)
Historical Landmark Series
Issued: 1997 • Retired: 1997
#58500 • Original Price: $165
Market Value: $365

DICKENS' VILLAGE
– BUILDINGS –

	Year Purchased	Price Paid	Value Of My Collection
81.			
82.			
83.			
84.			
85.			
86.			
PENCIL TOTALS			

87

Victoria Station
Issued: 1989 • Retired: 1998
#5574-3 • Original Price: $100
Market Value: $120

88

Whittlesbourne Church
Issued: 1994 • Retired: 1998
#5821-1 • Original Price: $85
Market Value: $92

89

Wrenbury Shops (set/3)
Issued: 1995 • Retired: 1997
#58331 • Original Price: $100
Market Value: $110

89a

The Chop Shop
Issued: 1995 • Retired: 1997
#58333 • Original Price: $35
Market Value: $40

89b

T. Puddlewick Spectacle Shop
Issued: 1995 • Retired: 1998
#58334 • Original Price: $35
Market Value: $40

89c

Wrenbury Baker
Issued: 1995 • Retired: 1997
#58332 • Original Price: $35
Market Value: $40

DICKENS' VILLAGE
– BUILDINGS –

	Year Purchased	Price Paid	Value Of My Collection
87.			
88.			
89.			
89a.			
89b.			
89c.			
PENCIL TOTALS			

NEW ENGLAND VILLAGE BUILDINGS

This collection of hometown favorites calls up memories of sledding, building snowmen and sipping hot cocoa by the fire. The village boasts 56 buildings, 13 of which are still current. "New England Village," an introductory set of seven buildings, was one of the first pieces to debut in 1986 and continues to be the most valuable on the secondary market.

NEW ENGLAND VILLAGE
– BUILDINGS –

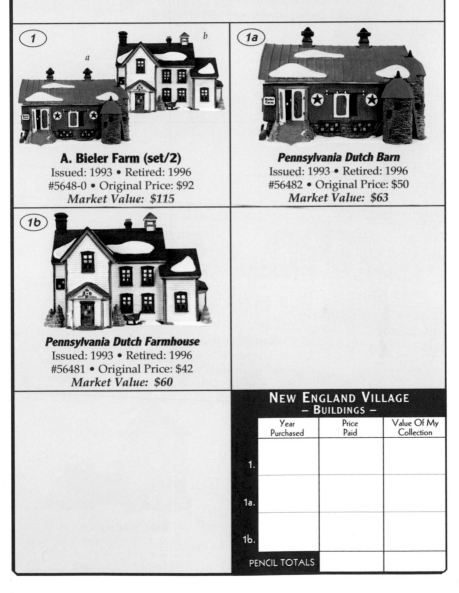

A. Bieler Farm (set/2)
Issued: 1993 • Retired: 1996
#5648-0 • Original Price: $92
Market Value: $115

Pennsylvania Dutch Barn
Issued: 1993 • Retired: 1996
#56482 • Original Price: $50
Market Value: $63

Pennsylvania Dutch Farmhouse
Issued: 1993 • Retired: 1996
#56481 • Original Price: $42
Market Value: $60

NEW ENGLAND VILLAGE
– BUILDINGS –

	Year Purchased	Price Paid	Value Of My Collection
1.			
1a.			
1b.			
PENCIL TOTALS			

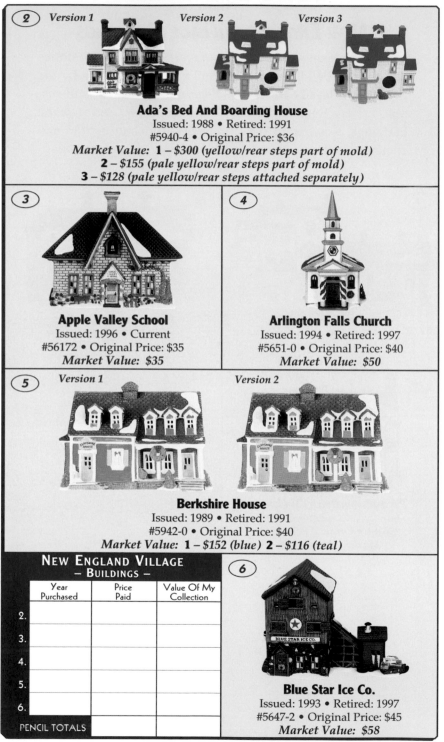

(2) Version 1   Version 2   Version 3

Ada's Bed And Boarding House
Issued: 1988 • Retired: 1991
#5940-4 • Original Price: $36
Market Value: **1** – *$300 (yellow/rear steps part of mold)*
2 – *$155 (pale yellow/rear steps part of mold)*
3 – *$128 (pale yellow/rear steps attached separately)*

(3)

Apple Valley School
Issued: 1996 • Current
#56172 • Original Price: $35
Market Value: $35

(4)

Arlington Falls Church
Issued: 1994 • Retired: 1997
#5651-0 • Original Price: $40
Market Value: $50

(5) Version 1   Version 2

Berkshire House
Issued: 1989 • Retired: 1991
#5942-0 • Original Price: $40
Market Value: **1** – *$152 (blue)* **2** – *$116 (teal)*

NEW ENGLAND VILLAGE
– BUILDINGS –

	Year Purchased	Price Paid	Value Of My Collection
2.			
3.			
4.			
5.			
6.			
PENCIL TOTALS			

(6)

Blue Star Ice Co.
Issued: 1993 • Retired: 1997
#5647-2 • Original Price: $45
Market Value: $58

(7)

Bluebird Seed And Bulb
Issued: 1992 • Retired: 1996
#5642-1 • Original Price: $48
Market Value: $60

(8)

Bobwhite Cottage
Issued: 1996 • Current
#56576 • Original Price: $50
Market Value: $50

(9)

a *b*

Brewster Bay Cottages (set/2)
Issued: 1995 • Retired: 1997
#5657-0 • Original Price: $90
Market Value: $100

(9a)

Jeremiah Brewster House
Issued: 1995 • Retired: 1997
#56568 • Original Price: $45
Market Value: $50

(9b)

Thomas T. Julian House
Issued: 1995 • Retired: 1997
#56569 • Original Price: $45
Market Value: $50

(10)

Cape Keag Fish Cannery
Issued: 1994 • Retired: 1998
#5652-9 • Original Price: $48
Market Value: $56

(11)

Captain's Cottage
Issued: 1990 • Retired: 1996
#5947-1 • Original Price: $40
Market Value: $60

NEW ENGLAND VILLAGE
– BUILDINGS –

	Year Purchased	Price Paid	Value Of My Collection
7.			
8.			
9.			
9a.			
9b.			
10.			
11.			
PENCIL TOTALS			

(side tab) **NEW ENGLAND VILLAGE – BUILDINGS –**

53

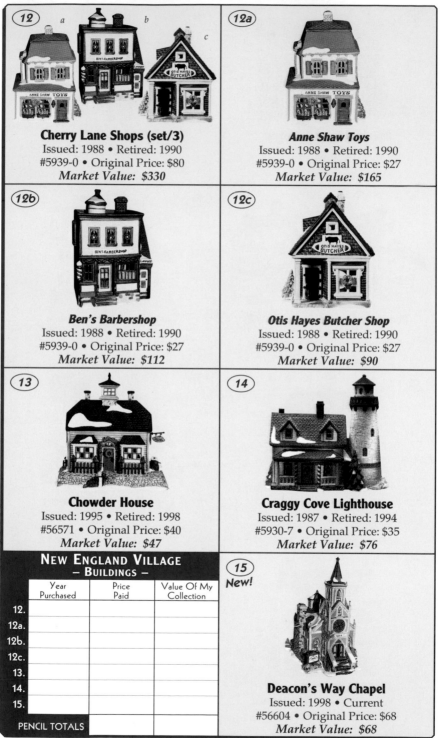

(12)

Cherry Lane Shops (set/3)
Issued: 1988 • Retired: 1990
#5939-0 • Original Price: $80
Market Value: $330

(12a)

Anne Shaw Toys
Issued: 1988 • Retired: 1990
#5939-0 • Original Price: $27
Market Value: $165

(12b)

Ben's Barbershop
Issued: 1988 • Retired: 1990
#5939-0 • Original Price: $27
Market Value: $112

(12c)

Otis Hayes Butcher Shop
Issued: 1988 • Retired: 1990
#5939-0 • Original Price: $27
Market Value: $90

(13)

Chowder House
Issued: 1995 • Retired: 1998
#56571 • Original Price: $40
Market Value: $47

(14)

Craggy Cove Lighthouse
Issued: 1987 • Retired: 1994
#5930-7 • Original Price: $35
Market Value: $76

NEW ENGLAND VILLAGE
– BUILDINGS –

	Year Purchased	Price Paid	Value Of My Collection
12.			
12a.			
12b.			
12c.			
13.			
14.			
15.			
PENCIL TOTALS			

(15)

New!

Deacon's Way Chapel
Issued: 1998 • Current
#56604 • Original Price: $68
Market Value: $68

NEW ENGLAND VILLAGE – BUILDINGS –

16

East Willet Pottery
Issued: 1997 • Current
#56578 • Original Price: $45
Market Value: $45

17

The Emily Louise (set/2)
Issued: 1998 • Current
#56581 • Original Price: $70
Market Value: $70

18
New!

Franklin Hook & Ladder Co.
Issued: 1998 • Current
#56601 • Original Price: $55
Market Value: $55

19
New!

Harper's Farm
Issued: 1998 • Current
#56605 • Original Price: $65
Market Value: $65

20

J. Hudson Stoveworks
Issued: 1996 • Retired: 1998
#56574 • Original Price: $60
Market Value: $70

21

**Jacob Adams Farmhouse
And Barn (set/5)**
Issued: 1986 • Retired: 1989
#6538-2 • Original Price: $65
Market Value: $540

22

Jannes Mullet Amish Barn
Issued: 1989 • Retired: 1992
#5944-7 • Original Price: $48
Market Value: $100

NEW ENGLAND VILLAGE
– BUILDINGS –

	Year Purchased	Price Paid	Value Of My Collection
16.			
17.			
18.			
19.			
20.			
21.			
22.			
PENCIL TOTALS			

(23)

Jannes Mullet Amish Farm House
Issued: 1989 • Retired: 1992
#5943-9 • Original Price: $32
Market Value: $120

(24)

McGrebe-Cutters & Sleighs
Issued: 1991 • Retired: 1995
#5640-5 • Original Price: $45
Market Value: $68

(25) New!

Moggin Falls General Store
Issued: 1998 • Current
#56602 • Original Price: $60
Market Value: $60

(26)

Navigational Charts & Maps
Issued: 1996 • Current
#56575 • Original Price: $48
Market Value: $48

(27) a b c d e f g

New England Village (set/7)
Issued: 1986 • Retired: 1989
#6530-7 • Original Price: $170
Market Value: **1** *– $1,220 (with Steeple Church version 1)*
2 *– $1,136 (with Steeple Church version 2)*

NEW ENGLAND VILLAGE
– BUILDINGS –

	Year Purchased	Price Paid	Value Of My Collection
23.			
24.			
25.			
26.			
27.			
27a.			
PENCIL TOTALS			

(27a)

Apothecary Shop
Issued: 1986 • Retired: 1989
#6530-7 • Original Price: $25
Market Value: $110

27b

Brick Town Hall
Issued: 1986 • Retired: 1989
#6530-7 • Original Price: $25
Market Value: $208

27c

General Store
Issued: 1986 • Retired: 1989
#6530-7 • Original Price: $25
Market Value: $320

27d

Livery Stable & Boot Shop
Issued: 1986 • Retired: 1989
#6530-7 • Original Price: $25
Market Value: $155

27e

Nathaniel Bingham Fabrics
Issued: 1986 • Retired: 1989
#6530-7 • Original Price: $25
Market Value: $175

27f

Red Schoolhouse
Issued: 1986 • Retired: 1989
#6530-7 • Original Price: $25
Market Value: $270

27g

Version 1   Version 2

Steeple Church
Issued: 1986 • Retired: 1989
#6530-7 • Original Price: $25
Market Value:
1 – $182 (tree attached with slip)
2 – $98 (tree attached with glue)

28

Old North Church
Issued: 1988 • Retired: 1998
#5932-3 • Original Price: $40
Market Value: $52

NEW ENGLAND VILLAGE
– BUILDINGS –

	Year Purchased	Price Paid	Value Of My Collection
27b.			
27c.			
27d.			
27e.			
27f.			
27g.			
28.			
PENCIL TOTALS			

NEW ENGLAND VILLAGE
– BUILDINGS –

29

Pierce Boat Works
Issued: 1995 • Current
#56573 • Original Price: $55
Market Value: $55

30

Pigeonhead Lighthouse
Issued: 1994 • Retired: 1998
#5653-7 • Original Price: $50
Market Value: $56

31

Semple's Smokehouse
Issued: 1997 • Current
#56580 • Original Price: $45
Market Value: $45

32

Shingle Creek House
Issued: 1990 • Retired: 1994
#5946-3 • Original Price: $37.50
Market Value: $62

33

Sleepy Hollow (set/3)
Issued: 1990 • Retired: 1993
#5954-4 • Original Price: $96
Market Value: $200

33a

Ichabod Crane's Cottage
Issued: 1990 • Retired: 1993
#5954-4 • Original Price: $32
Market Value: $59

NEW ENGLAND VILLAGE
– BUILDINGS –

	Year Purchased	Price Paid	Value Of My Collection
29.			
30.			
31.			
32.			
33.			
33a.			
33b.			
PENCIL TOTALS			

33b

Sleepy Hollow School
Issued: 1990 • Retired: 1993
#5954-4 • Original Price: $32
Market Value: $100

NEW ENGLAND VILLAGE
– BUILDINGS –

(33c)

Van Tassel Manor
Issued: 1990 • Retired: 1993
#5954-4 • Original Price: $32
Market Value: $63

(34)

Sleepy Hollow Church
Issued: 1990 • Retired: 1993
#5955-2 • Original Price: $36
Market Value: $70

(35)

Smythe Woolen Mill (LE-7,500)
Issued: 1987 • Retired: 1988
#6543-9 • Original Price: $42
Market Value: $1,100

(36)

**Steen's Maple House
(with magic smoking element)**
Issued: 1997 • Current
#56579 • Original Price: $60
Market Value: $60

(37)

Steeple Church
Issued: 1986 • Retired: 1990
#6539-0 • Original Price: $30
Market Value: $93

(38)

Stoney Brook Town Hall
Issued: 1992 • Retired: 1995
#5644-8 • Original Price: $42
Market Value: $66

(39)

Timber Knoll Log Cabin
Issued: 1987 • Retired: 1990
#6544-7 • Original Price: $28
Market Value: $185

NEW ENGLAND VILLAGE
– BUILDINGS –

	Year Purchased	Price Paid	Value Of My Collection
33c.			
34.			
35.			
36.			
37.			
38.			
39.			
PENCIL TOTALS			

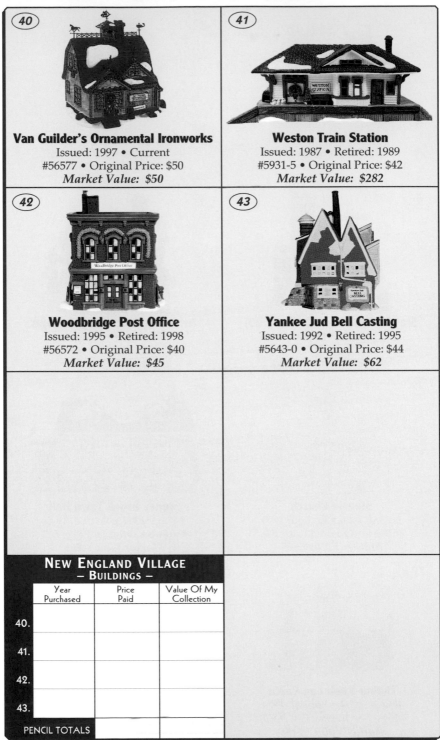

40

Van Guilder's Ornamental Ironworks
Issued: 1997 • Current
#56577 • Original Price: $50
Market Value: $50

41

Weston Train Station
Issued: 1987 • Retired: 1989
#5931-5 • Original Price: $42
Market Value: $282

42

Woodbridge Post Office
Issued: 1995 • Retired: 1998
#56572 • Original Price: $40
Market Value: $45

43

Yankee Jud Bell Casting
Issued: 1992 • Retired: 1995
#5643-0 • Original Price: $44
Market Value: $62

NEW ENGLAND VILLAGE
– BUILDINGS –

	Year Purchased	Price Paid	Value Of My Collection
40.			
41.			
42.			
43.			
PENCIL TOTALS			

ALPINE VILLAGE BUILDINGS

Since 1986 Department 56 collectors have celebrated the holiday season with the people of the European mountain town known as *Alpine Village*. While it may be small in size with only 21 buildings, this village stands can't be missed with its bright, colorful facades. Many of the buildings are named in German, while a few pieces have English titles, including the most valuable piece, "Joseph Engel Farmhouse."

ALPINE VILLAGE – BUILDINGS –

(1)   Version 1   Version 2

Alpine Church
Issued: 1987 • Retired: 1991
#6541-2 • Original Price: $32
Market Value: **1** – $430 *(white trim)* **2** – $178 *(brown trim)*

(2)   a   b

Alpine Shops (set/2)
Issued: 1992 • Retired: 1997
#5618-9 • Original Price: $75
Market Value: $85

(2a)

Kukuck Uhren
Issued: 1992 • Retired: 1998
#56191 • Original Price: $37.50
Market Value: $40

(2b)

Metterniche Wurst
Issued: 1992 • Retired: 1997
#56190 • Original Price: $37.50
Market Value: $45

ALPINE VILLAGE – BUILDINGS –

	Year Purchased	Price Paid	Value Of My Collection
1.			
2.			
2a.			
2b.			
PENCIL TOTALS			

3 a   b

c

d

e

Alpine Village (set/5)
Issued: 1986 • Retired: 1996
#6540-4 • Original Price: $150
Market Value: $187

3a

Apotheke
Issued: 1986 • Retired: 1997
#65407 • Original Price: $25
Market Value: $44

3b

Besson Bierkeller
Issued: 1986 • Retired: 1996
#65405 • Original Price: $25
Market Value: $48

3c

E. Staubr Backer
Issued: 1986 • Retired: 1997
#65408 • Original Price: $25
Market Value: $44

3d

Gasthof Eisl
Issued: 1986 • Retired: 1996
#65406 • Original Price: $25
Market Value: $46

3e

Milch-Kase
Issued: 1986 • Retired: 1996
#65409 • Original Price: $25
Market Value: $48

ALPINE VILLAGE
– BUILDINGS –

	Year Purchased	Price Paid	Value Of My Collection
3.			
3a.			
3b.			
3c.			
3d.			
3e.			
4.			
PENCIL TOTALS			

4

Bahnhof
Issued: 1990 • Retired: 1993
#5615-4 • Original Price: $42
Market Value: $85

ALPINE VILLAGE
– BUILDINGS –

5

Bakery & Chocolate Shop (Konditorei Schokolade)
Issued: 1994 • Retired: 1998
#5614-6 • Original Price: $37.50
Market Value: $40

6

Bernhardiner Hundchen (St. Bernard Puppies)
Issued: 1997 • Current
#56174 • Original Price: $50
Market Value: $50

7

Danube Music Publisher
Issued: 1996 • Current
#56173 • Original Price: $55
Market Value: $55

8

Federbetten Und Steppdecken
Issued: 1998 • Current
#56176 • Orig. Price: $48
Market Value: $48

9

Grist Mill
Issued: 1988 • Retired: 1997
#5953-6 • Original Price: $42
Market Value: $54

10
New!

Heidi's Grandfather's House
Issued: 1998 • Current
#56177 • Original Price: $64
Market Value: $64

11

Josef Engel Farmhouse
Issued: 1987 • Retired: 1989
#5952-8 • Original Price: $33
Market Value: $1,030

ALPINE VILLAGE
– BUILDINGS –

	Year Purchased	Price Paid	Value Of My Collection
5.			
6.			
7.			
8.			
9.			
10.			
11.			
PENCIL TOTALS			

12

Kamm Haus
Issued: 1995 • Current
#56171 • Original Price: $42
Market Value: $42

13

St. Nikolaus Kirche
Issued: 1991 • Current
#5617-0 • Original Price: $37.50
Market Value: $37.50

14
New!

**The Sound Of Music®
von Trapp Villa (set/5)**
Issued: 1998 • Current
#56178 • Orig. Price: $130
Market Value: $130

15

Spielzeug Laden
Issued: 1997 • Current
#56192 • Original Price: $65
Market Value: $65

16

Sport Laden
Issued: 1993 • Retired: 1998
#5612-0 • Original Price: $50
Market Value: $55

ALPINE VILLAGE
– BUILDINGS –

	Year Purchased	Price Paid	Value Of My Collection
12.			
13.			
14.			
15.			
16.			
PENCIL TOTALS			

CHRISTMAS IN THE CITY BUILDINGS

Carriage rides, hot dog vendors on the street corner and window shopping are all brought to life in the *Christmas in the City* village. To date, there are 49 buildings, with only 13 currently available. With everything from three-story brownstones to corner cafes, these pieces are perfect replicas of big city buildings that will ensure you can build the perfect thriving metropolis right in your own home.

(1) **5607 Park Avenue Townhouse** Issued: 1989 • Retired: 1992 #5977-3 • Original Price: $48 *Market Value: $94*	**(2)** **5609 Park Avenue Townhouse** Issued: 1989 • Retired: 1992 #5978-1 • Original Price: $48 *Market Value: $94*

(3)

All Saints Corner Church
Issued: 1991 • Retired: 1998
#5542-5 • Original Price: $96
Market Value: $116

(4)

Arts Academy
Issued: 1991 • Retired: 1993
#5543-3 • Original Price: $45
Market Value: $83

(5)

Brighton School
Issued: 1995 • Retired: 1998
#58876 • Original Price: $52
Market Value: $56

CHRISTMAS IN THE CITY
— BUILDINGS —

	Year Purchased	Price Paid	Value Of My Collection
1.			
2.			
3.			
4.			
5.			
PENCIL TOTALS			

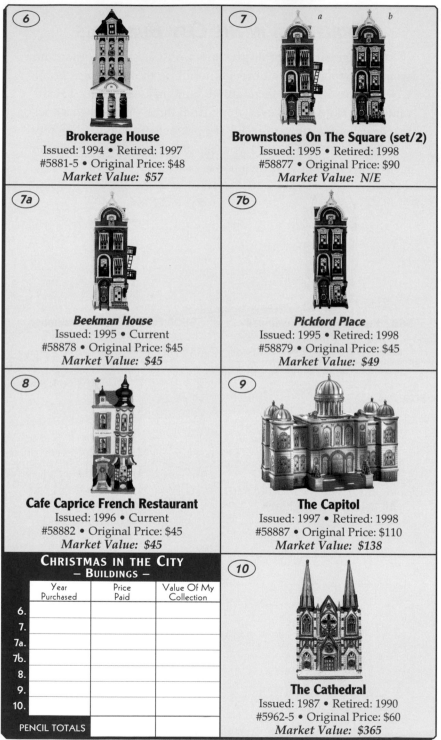

6

Brokerage House
Issued: 1994 • Retired: 1997
#5881-5 • Original Price: $48
Market Value: $57

7 *a* *b*

Brownstones On The Square (set/2)
Issued: 1995 • Retired: 1998
#58877 • Original Price: $90
Market Value: N/E

7a

Beekman House
Issued: 1995 • Current
#58878 • Original Price: $45
Market Value: $45

7b

Pickford Place
Issued: 1995 • Retired: 1998
#58879 • Original Price: $45
Market Value: $49

8

Cafe Caprice French Restaurant
Issued: 1996 • Current
#58882 • Original Price: $45
Market Value: $45

9

The Capitol
Issued: 1997 • Retired: 1998
#58887 • Original Price: $110
Market Value: $138

CHRISTMAS IN THE CITY
– BUILDINGS –

	Year Purchased	Price Paid	Value Of My Collection
6.			
7.			
7a.			
7b.			
8.			
9.			
10.			
PENCIL TOTALS			

10

The Cathedral
Issued: 1987 • Retired: 1990
#5962-5 • Original Price: $60
Market Value: $365

11

Cathedral Church Of St. Mark (LE-3,024)
Issued: 1991 • Retired: 1993
#5549-2 • Original Price: $120
Market Value: $2,100

12

Chocolate Shoppe
Issued: 1988 • Retired: 1991
#5968-4 • Original Price: $40
Market Value: $152

13 *a* *b* *c*

Christmas In The City (set/3)
Issued: 1987 • Retired: 1990
#6512-9 • Original Price: $112
Market Value: $620

13a

Bakery
Issued: 1987 • Retired: 1990
#6512-9 • Original Price: $37.50
Market Value: $132

13b

Tower Restaurant
Issued: 1987 • Retired: 1990
#6512-9 • Original Price: $37.50
Market Value: $270

13c

Toy Shop And Pet Store
Issued: 1987 • Retired: 1990
#6512-9 • Original Price: $37.50
Market Value: $270

14

The City Globe
Issued: 1997 • Current
#58883 • Original Price: $65
Market Value: $65

CHRISTMAS IN THE CITY
– BUILDINGS –

	Year Purchased	Price Paid	Value Of My Collection
11.			
12.			
13.			
13a.			
13b.			
13c.			
14.			
PENCIL TOTALS			

CHRISTMAS IN THE CITY
– BUILDINGS –

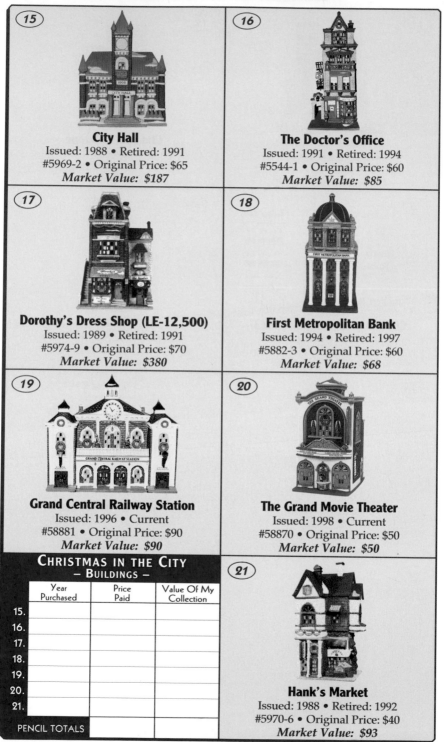

15

City Hall
Issued: 1988 • Retired: 1991
#5969-2 • Original Price: $65
Market Value: $187

16

The Doctor's Office
Issued: 1991 • Retired: 1994
#5544-1 • Original Price: $60
Market Value: $85

17

Dorothy's Dress Shop (LE-12,500)
Issued: 1989 • Retired: 1991
#5974-9 • Original Price: $70
Market Value: $380

18

First Metropolitan Bank
Issued: 1994 • Retired: 1997
#5882-3 • Original Price: $60
Market Value: $68

19

Grand Central Railway Station
Issued: 1996 • Current
#58881 • Original Price: $90
Market Value: $90

20

The Grand Movie Theater
Issued: 1998 • Current
#58870 • Original Price: $50
Market Value: $50

CHRISTMAS IN THE CITY
– BUILDINGS –

	Year Purchased	Price Paid	Value Of My Collection
15.			
16.			
17.			
18.			
19.			
20.			
21.			
PENCIL TOTALS			

21

Hank's Market
Issued: 1988 • Retired: 1992
#5970-6 • Original Price: $40
Market Value: $93

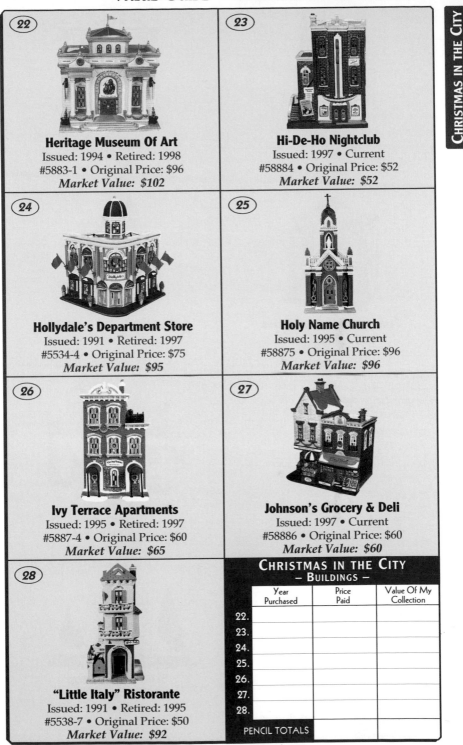

22

Heritage Museum Of Art
Issued: 1994 • Retired: 1998
#5883-1 • Original Price: $96
Market Value: $102

23

Hi-De-Ho Nightclub
Issued: 1997 • Current
#58884 • Original Price: $52
Market Value: $52

24

Hollydale's Department Store
Issued: 1991 • Retired: 1997
#5534-4 • Original Price: $75
Market Value: $95

25

Holy Name Church
Issued: 1995 • Current
#58875 • Original Price: $96
Market Value: $96

26

Ivy Terrace Apartments
Issued: 1995 • Retired: 1997
#5887-4 • Original Price: $60
Market Value: $65

27

Johnson's Grocery & Deli
Issued: 1997 • Current
#58886 • Original Price: $60
Market Value: $60

28

"Little Italy" Ristorante
Issued: 1991 • Retired: 1995
#5538-7 • Original Price: $50
Market Value: $92

CHRISTMAS IN THE CITY
– BUILDINGS –

	Year Purchased	Price Paid	Value Of My Collection
22.			
23.			
24.			
25.			
26.			
27.			
28.			
PENCIL TOTALS			

CHRISTMAS IN THE CITY – BUILDINGS –

(29) New!

Old Trinity Church
Issued: 1998 • Current
#58940 • Original Price: $96
Market Value: $96

(30)

Palace Theatre
Issued: 1987 • Retired: 1989
#5963-3 • Original Price: $45
Market Value: $955

(31) New!

Precinct 25 Police Station
Issued: 1998 • Current
#58941 • Original Price: $56
Market Value: $56

(32)

Red Brick Fire Station
Issued: 1990 • Retired: 1995
#5536-0 • Original Price: $55
Market Value: $88

(33)

Ritz Hotel
Issued: 1989 • Retired: 1994
#5973-0 • Original Price: $55
Market Value: $82

(34)

Riverside Row Shops
Issued: 1997 • Current
#58888 • Original Price: $52
Market Value: $52

CHRISTMAS IN THE CITY
– BUILDINGS –

	Year Purchased	Price Paid	Value Of My Collection
29.			
30.			
31.			
32.			
33.			
34.			
35.			
PENCIL TOTALS			

(35)

Scottie's Toy Shop

5¢ Pony Rides

Scottie's Toy Shop
(set/10, Event Piece)
Issued: 1998 • Retired: 1998
#58871 • Orig. Price: $65
Market Value: $98

36

Sutton Place Brownstones
Issued: 1987 • Retired: 1989
#5961-7 • Original Price: $80
Market Value: $900

37
New!

The University Club
Issued: 1998 • Current
#58945 • Original Price: $60
Market Value: $60

38   a   b   c

Uptown Shoppes (set/3)
Issued: 1992 • Retired: 1996
#5531-0 • Original Price: $150
Market Value: $182

38a

City Clockworks
Issued: 1992 • Retired: 1996
#55313 • Original Price: $56
Market Value: $68

38b

Haberdashery
Issued: 1992 • Retired: 1996
#55311 • Original Price: $40
Market Value: $56

38c

Music Emporium
Issued: 1992 • Retired: 1996
#55312 • Original Price: $54
Market Value: $67

39

Variety Store
Issued: 1988 • Retired: 1990
#5972-2 • Original Price: $45
Market Value: $189

CHRISTMAS IN THE CITY
— BUILDINGS —

	Year Purchased	Price Paid	Value Of My Collection
36.			
37.			
38.			
38a.			
38b.			
38c.			
39.			
PENCIL TOTALS			

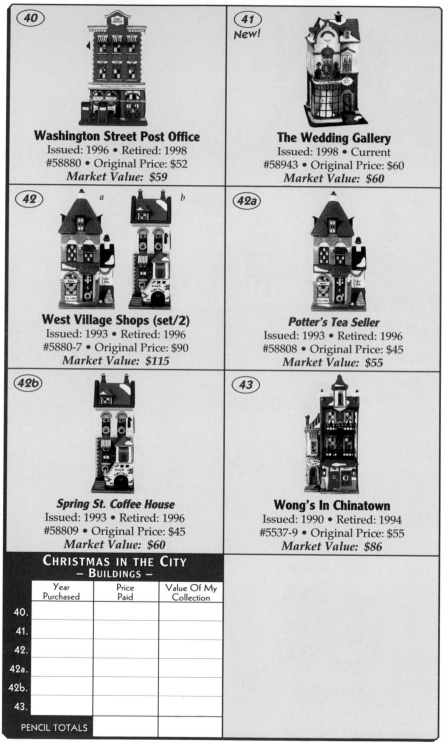

(40)

Washington Street Post Office
Issued: 1996 • Retired: 1998
#58880 • Original Price: $52
Market Value: $59

(41) New!

The Wedding Gallery
Issued: 1998 • Current
#58943 • Original Price: $60
Market Value: $60

(42) a b

West Village Shops (set/2)
Issued: 1993 • Retired: 1996
#5880-7 • Original Price: $90
Market Value: $115

(42a)

Potter's Tea Seller
Issued: 1993 • Retired: 1996
#58808 • Original Price: $45
Market Value: $55

(42b)

Spring St. Coffee House
Issued: 1993 • Retired: 1996
#58809 • Original Price: $45
Market Value: $60

(43)

Wong's In Chinatown
Issued: 1990 • Retired: 1994
#5537-9 • Original Price: $55
Market Value: $86

CHRISTMAS IN THE CITY
– BUILDINGS –

	Year Purchased	Price Paid	Value Of My Collection
40.			
41.			
42.			
42a.			
42b.			
43.			
PENCIL TOTALS			

NORTH POLE BUILDINGS

From the "Reindeer Flight School" to "Mrs. Claus' Greenhouse," this village represents every aspect of life at the *North Pole*. The collection, which came to life in 1990, consists of 40 buildings, 22 of which have been retired. To date, "Santa's Workshop" is the most valuable *North Pole* piece on the secondary market. An exciting new addition to the *North Pole* this year is the *Elf Land* series.

(1)

Beard Barber Shop
Issued: 1994 • Retired: 1997
#5634-0 • Original Price: $27.50
Market Value: $38

(2)

Christmas Bread Bakers
Issued: 1996 • Current
#56393 • Original Price: $55
Market Value: $55

(3) New!

Custom Stitchers
Elf Land
Issued: 1998 • Current
#56400 • Original Price: $37.50
Market Value: $37.50

(4) New!

The Elf Spa
Elf Land
Issued: 1998 • Current
#56402 • Original Price: $40
Market Value: $40

(5)

Elfie's Sleds & Skates
Issued: 1992 • Retired: 1996
#5625-1 • Original Price: $48
Market Value: $64

NORTH POLE
– BUILDINGS –

	Year Purchased	Price Paid	Value Of My Collection
1.			
2.			
3.			
4.			
5.			
PENCIL TOTALS			

NORTH POLE – BUILDINGS –

(6)

Elfin Forge & Assembly Shop
Issued: 1995 • Retired: 1998
#56384 • Original Price: $65
Market Value: $70

(7)

Elfin Snow Cone Works
Issued: 1994 • Retired: 1997
#5633-2 • Original Price: $40
Market Value: $47

(8)

Elsie's Gingerbread (with magic smoking element, LE–1998)
Issued: 1997 • Retired: 1998
#56398 • Original Price: $65
Market Value: $105

(9)

Elves' Trade School
Issued: 1995 • Retired: 1998
#56387 • Original Price: $50
Market Value: $55

(10)

The Glacier Gazette
Issued: 1997 • Current
#56394 • Original Price: $48
Market Value: $48

(11)

Glass Ornament Works
Issued: 1997 • Current
#56396 • Original Price: $60
Market Value: $60

NORTH POLE
– BUILDINGS –

	Year Purchased	Price Paid	Value Of My Collection
6.			
7.			
8.			
9.			
10.			
11.			
12.			
PENCIL TOTALS			

(12)

Hall Of Records
Issued: 1996 • Current
#56392 • Original Price: $50
Market Value: $50

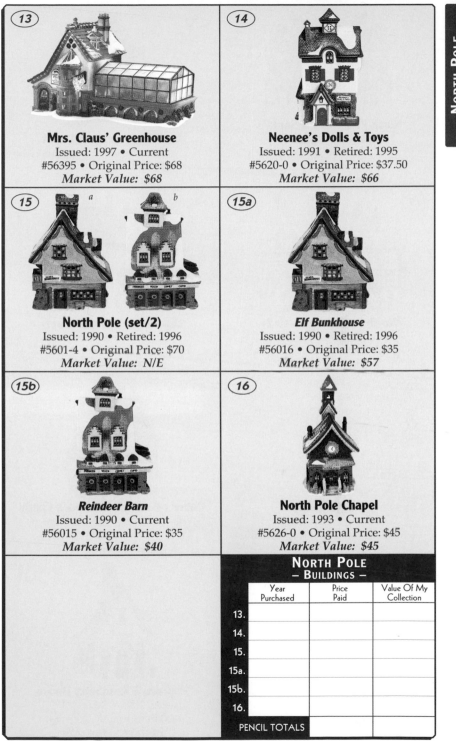

13

Mrs. Claus' Greenhouse
Issued: 1997 • Current
#56395 • Original Price: $68
Market Value: $68

14

Neenee's Dolls & Toys
Issued: 1991 • Retired: 1995
#5620-0 • Original Price: $37.50
Market Value: $66

15

a   b

North Pole (set/2)
Issued: 1990 • Retired: 1996
#5601-4 • Original Price: $70
Market Value: N/E

15a

Elf Bunkhouse
Issued: 1990 • Retired: 1996
#56016 • Original Price: $35
Market Value: $57

15b

Reindeer Barn
Issued: 1990 • Current
#56015 • Original Price: $35
Market Value: $40

16

North Pole Chapel
Issued: 1993 • Current
#5626-0 • Original Price: $45
Market Value: $45

NORTH POLE
– BUILDINGS –

	Year Purchased	Price Paid	Value Of My Collection
13.			
14.			
15.			
15a.			
15b.			
16.			
PENCIL TOTALS			

NORTH POLE – BUILDINGS –

17

North Pole Dolls   *Santa's Bear Works*

Entrance

North Pole Dolls & Santa's Bear Works (set/3)
Issued: 1994 • Retired: 1997
#5635-9 • Original Price: $96
Market Value: $103

18

North Pole Express Depot
Issued: 1993 • Retired: 1998
#5627-8 • Original Price: $48
Market Value: $54

19   *a*   *b*

North Pole Shops (set/2)
Issued: 1991 • Retired: 1995
#5621-9 • Original Price: $75
Market Value: $133

19a

Orly's Bell & Harness Supply
Issued: 1991 • Retired: 1995
#5621-9 • Original Price: $37.50
Market Value: $68

19b

Rimpy's Bakery
Issued: 1991 • Retired: 1995
#5621-9 • Original Price: $37.50
Market Value: $73

20

Obbie's Books & Letrinka's Candy
Issued: 1992 • Retired: 1996
#5624-3 • Original Price: $70
Market Value: $88

NORTH POLE
– BUILDINGS –

	Year Purchased	Price Paid	Value Of My Collection
17.			
18.			
19.			
19a.			
19b.			
20.			
21.			
PENCIL TOTALS			

21

Popcorn & Cranberry House
Issued: 1996 • Retired: 1997
#56388 • Original Price: $45
Market Value: $90

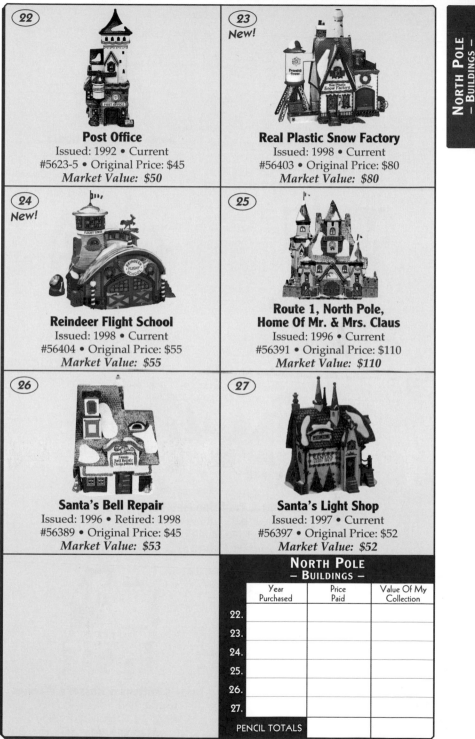

NORTH POLE
– BUILDINGS –

22

Post Office
Issued: 1992 • Current
#5623-5 • Original Price: $45
Market Value: $50

23
New!

Real Plastic Snow Factory
Issued: 1998 • Current
#56403 • Original Price: $80
Market Value: $80

24
New!

Reindeer Flight School
Issued: 1998 • Current
#56404 • Original Price: $55
Market Value: $55

25

Route 1, North Pole,
Home Of Mr. & Mrs. Claus
Issued: 1996 • Current
#56391 • Original Price: $110
Market Value: $110

26

Santa's Bell Repair
Issued: 1996 • Retired: 1998
#56389 • Original Price: $45
Market Value: $53

27

Santa's Light Shop
Issued: 1997 • Current
#56397 • Original Price: $52
Market Value: $52

NORTH POLE
– BUILDINGS –

	Year Purchased	Price Paid	Value Of My Collection
22.			
23.			
24.			
25.			
26.			
27.			
PENCIL TOTALS			

(28)

Santa's Lookout Tower
Issued: 1993 • Current
#5629-4 • Original Price: $45
Market Value: $48

(29)

Santa's Rooming House
Issued: 1995 • Current
#56386 • Original Price: $50
Market Value: $50

(30)

Santa's Woodworks
Issued: 1993 • Retired: 1996
#5628-6 • Original Price: $42
Market Value: $62

(31)

Santa's Workshop
Issued: 1990 • Retired: 1993
#5600-6 • Original Price: $72
Market Value: $445

(32)

*Gift Wrap &
Ribbons*

*Candy Cane &
Peppermint Shop*

*Candy Cane
Lane (set/2)*

Candy Cane Elves (set/2)

Start A Tradition (set/12)
Issued: 1996 • Retired: 1996
#56390 • Original Price: $85
Market Value: $112

NORTH POLE
– BUILDINGS –

	Year Purchased	Price Paid	Value Of My Collection
28.			
29.			
30.			
31.			
32.			
33.			
PENCIL TOTALS			

(33)

Tassy's Mittens & Hassel's Woolies
Issued: 1991 • Retired: 1995
#5622-7 • Original Price: $50
Market Value: $87

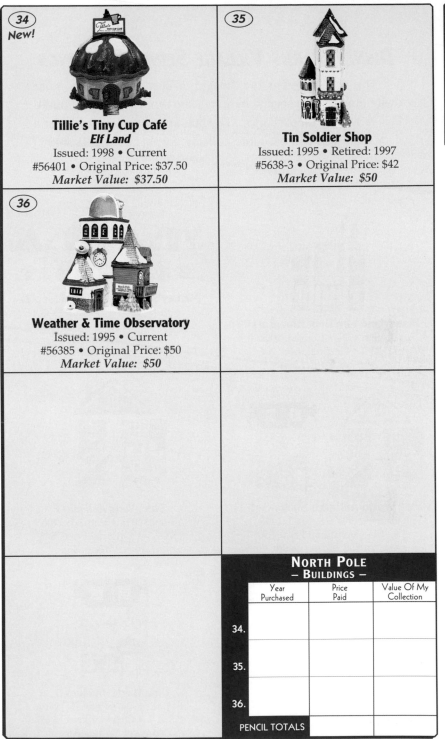

(34)
New!

Tillie's Tiny Cup Café
Elf Land
Issued: 1998 • Current
#56401 • Original Price: $37.50
Market Value: $37.50

(35)

Tin Soldier Shop
Issued: 1995 • Retired: 1997
#5638-3 • Original Price: $42
Market Value: $50

(36)

Weather & Time Observatory
Issued: 1995 • Current
#56385 • Original Price: $50
Market Value: $50

NORTH POLE
– BUILDINGS –

	Year Purchased	Price Paid	Value Of My Collection
34.			
35.			
36.			
PENCIL TOTALS			

NORTH POLE – BUILDINGS –

DISNEY PARKS VILLAGE SERIES BUILDINGS

This village brings the "magic of Disney" right into your own home. These special buildings are replicas of actual buildings at Disney theme parks. The buildings were available for a very short time and the entire collection was retired in 1996.

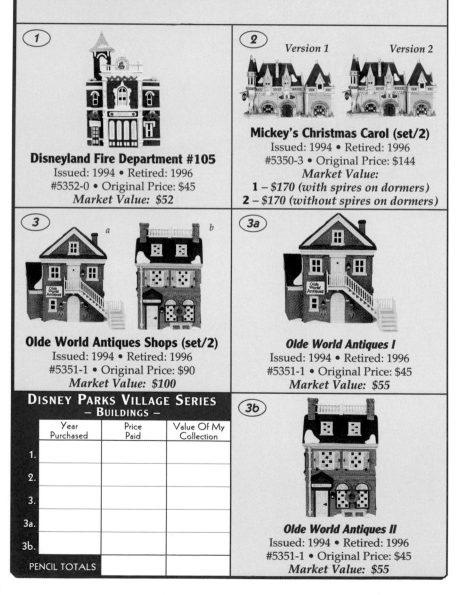

(1)

Disneyland Fire Department #105
Issued: 1994 • Retired: 1996
#5352-0 • Original Price: $45
Market Value: $52

(2) Version 1   Version 2

Mickey's Christmas Carol (set/2)
Issued: 1994 • Retired: 1996
#5350-3 • Original Price: $144
Market Value:
1 – $170 *(with spires on dormers)*
2 – $170 *(without spires on dormers)*

(3) a   b

Olde World Antiques Shops (set/2)
Issued: 1994 • Retired: 1996
#5351-1 • Original Price: $90
Market Value: $100

(3a)

Olde World Antiques I
Issued: 1994 • Retired: 1996
#5351-1 • Original Price: $45
Market Value: $55

(3b)

Olde World Antiques II
Issued: 1994 • Retired: 1996
#5351-1 • Original Price: $45
Market Value: $55

DISNEY PARKS VILLAGE SERIES
– BUILDINGS –

	Year Purchased	Price Paid	Value Of My Collection
1.			
2.			
3.			
3a.			
3b.			
PENCIL TOTALS			

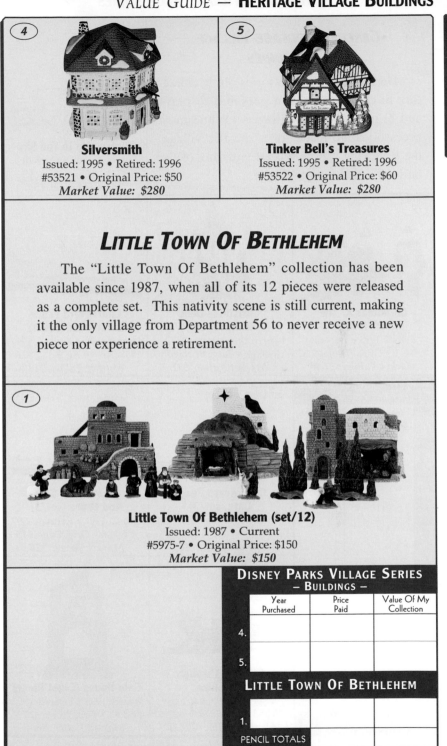

(4)

Silversmith
Issued: 1995 • Retired: 1996
#53521 • Original Price: $50
Market Value: $280

(5)

Tinker Bell's Treasures
Issued: 1995 • Retired: 1996
#53522 • Original Price: $60
Market Value: $280

LITTLE TOWN OF BETHLEHEM

The "Little Town Of Bethlehem" collection has been available since 1987, when all of its 12 pieces were released as a complete set. This nativity scene is still current, making it the only village from Department 56 to never receive a new piece nor experience a retirement.

(1)

Little Town Of Bethlehem (set/12)
Issued: 1987 • Current
#5975-7 • Original Price: $150
Market Value: $150

DISNEY PARKS VILLAGE SERIES
– BUILDINGS –

	Year Purchased	Price Paid	Value Of My Collection
4.			
5.			

LITTLE TOWN OF BETHLEHEM

1.			
PENCIL TOTALS			

GENERAL HERITAGE VILLAGE ACCESSORIES

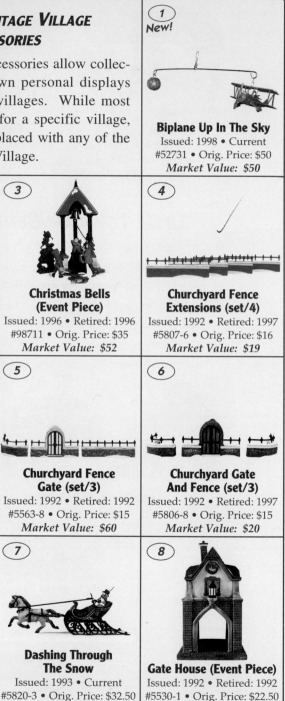

① New!

Department 56 accessories allow collectors to create their own personal displays and bring life to the villages. While most accessories are made for a specific village, the following can be placed with any of the buildings in Heritage Village.

Biplane Up In The Sky
Issued: 1998 • Current
#52731 • Orig. Price: $50
Market Value: $50

②

Christmas At The Park (set/3)
Issued: 1993 • Current
#5866-1 • Orig. Price: $27.50
Market Value: $27.50

③

Christmas Bells (Event Piece)
Issued: 1996 • Retired: 1996
#98711 • Orig. Price: $35
Market Value: $52

④

Churchyard Fence Extensions (set/4)
Issued: 1992 • Retired: 1997
#5807-6 • Orig. Price: $16
Market Value: $19

GENERAL HERITAGE VILLAGE – ACCESSORIES –

	Year Purch.	Price Paid	Value Of My Collection
1.			
2.			
3.			
4.			
5.			
6.			
7.			
8.			
PENCIL TOTALS			

⑤

Churchyard Fence Gate (set/3)
Issued: 1992 • Retired: 1992
#5563-8 • Orig. Price: $15
Market Value: $60

⑥

Churchyard Gate And Fence (set/3)
Issued: 1992 • Retired: 1997
#5806-8 • Orig. Price: $15
Market Value: $20

⑦

Dashing Through The Snow
Issued: 1993 • Current
#5820-3 • Orig. Price: $32.50
Market Value: $32.50

⑧

Gate House (Event Piece)
Issued: 1992 • Retired: 1992
#5530-1 • Orig. Price: $22.50
Market Value: $60

9 Heritage Village Promotional Sign
Issued: 1989 • Retired: 1990
#9953-8 • Orig. Price: $5
Market Value: $30

10 The Holly & The Ivy (set/2, Event Piece)
Issued: 1997 • Retired: 1997
#56100 • Orig. Price: $17.50
Market Value: $33

11 Lighted Tree w/Children And Ladder (set/3)
Issued: 1986 • Retired: 1989
#6510-2 • Orig. Price: $35
Market Value: $320

GENERAL HERITAGE VILLAGE – ACCESSORIES –

12 One Horse Open Sleigh
Issued: 1988 • Retired: 1993
#5982-0 • Orig. Price: $20
Market Value: $42

13 New!
Painting Our Own Village Sign
Issued: 1998 • Current
#55501 • Orig. Price: $12.50
Market Value: $12.50

14 Playing In The Snow (set/3)
Issued: 1993 • Retired: 1996
#5556-5 • Orig. Price: $25
Market Value: $33

15 Version 1   Version 2

PHOTO UNAVAILABLE

Poinsettia Delivery Truck
Issued: 1997 • Current
#59000 • Orig. Price: $32.50
Market Value:
1 – $32.50 (general release) 2 – N/E (William Glen)

16 Porcelain Trees (set/2)
Issued: 1986 • Retired: 1992
#6537-4 • Orig. Price: $14
Market Value: $42

	Year Purch.	Price Paid	Value Of My Collection
9.			
10.			
11.			
12.			
13.			
14.			
15.			
16.			
PENCIL TOTALS			

GENERAL HERITAGE VILLAGE – ACCESSORIES –

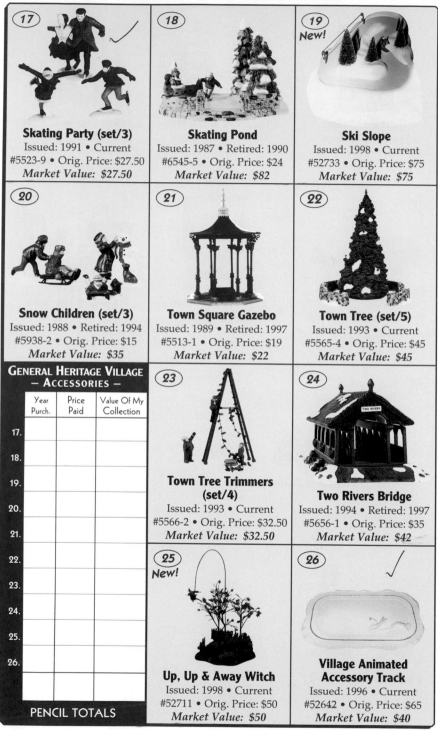

17

Skating Party (set/3)
Issued: 1991 • Current
#5523-9 • Orig. Price: $27.50
Market Value: $27.50

18

Skating Pond
Issued: 1987 • Retired: 1990
#6545-5 • Orig. Price: $24
Market Value: $82

19
New!

Ski Slope
Issued: 1998 • Current
#52733 • Orig. Price: $75
Market Value: $75

20

Snow Children (set/3)
Issued: 1988 • Retired: 1994
#5938-2 • Orig. Price: $15
Market Value: $35

21

Town Square Gazebo
Issued: 1989 • Retired: 1997
#5513-1 • Orig. Price: $19
Market Value: $22

22

Town Tree (set/5)
Issued: 1993 • Current
#5565-4 • Orig. Price: $45
Market Value: $45

**GENERAL HERITAGE VILLAGE
– ACCESSORIES –**

	Year Purch.	Price Paid	Value Of My Collection
17.			
18.			
19.			
20.			
21.			
22.			
23.			
24.			
25.			
26.			
PENCIL TOTALS			

23

Town Tree Trimmers (set/4)
Issued: 1993 • Current
#5566-2 • Orig. Price: $32.50
Market Value: $32.50

24

Two Rivers Bridge
Issued: 1994 • Retired: 1997
#5656-1 • Orig. Price: $35
Market Value: $42

25
New!

Up, Up & Away Witch
Issued: 1998 • Current
#52711 • Orig. Price: $50
Market Value: $50

26

Village Animated Accessory Track
Issued: 1996 • Current
#52642 • Orig. Price: $65
Market Value: $40

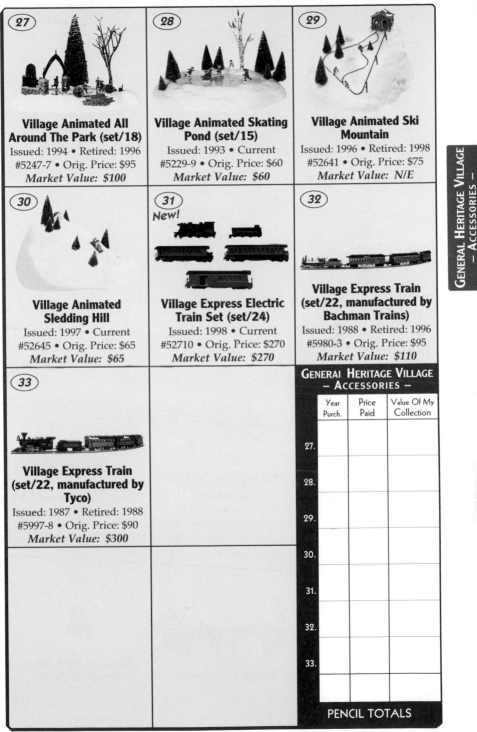

(27)

Village Animated All Around The Park (set/18)
Issued: 1994 • Retired: 1996
#5247-7 • Orig. Price: $95
Market Value: $100

(28)

Village Animated Skating Pond (set/15)
Issued: 1993 • Current
#5229-9 • Orig. Price: $60
Market Value: $60

(29)

Village Animated Ski Mountain
Issued: 1996 • Retired: 1998
#52641 • Orig. Price: $75
Market Value: N/E

(30)

Village Animated Sledding Hill
Issued: 1997 • Current
#52645 • Orig. Price: $65
Market Value: $65

(31)
New!

Village Express Electric Train Set (set/24)
Issued: 1998 • Current
#52710 • Orig. Price: $270
Market Value: $270

(32)

Village Express Train (set/22, manufactured by Bachman Trains)
Issued: 1988 • Retired: 1996
#5980-3 • Orig. Price: $95
Market Value: $110

(33)

Village Express Train (set/22, manufactured by Tyco)
Issued: 1987 • Retired: 1988
#5997-8 • Orig. Price: $90
Market Value: $300

GENERAL HERITAGE VILLAGE – ACCESSORIES –

	Year Purch.	Price Paid	Value Of My Collection
27.			
28.			
29.			
30.			
31.			
32.			
33.			
PENCIL TOTALS			

(sidebar:) **GENERAL HERITAGE VILLAGE – ACCESSORIES –**

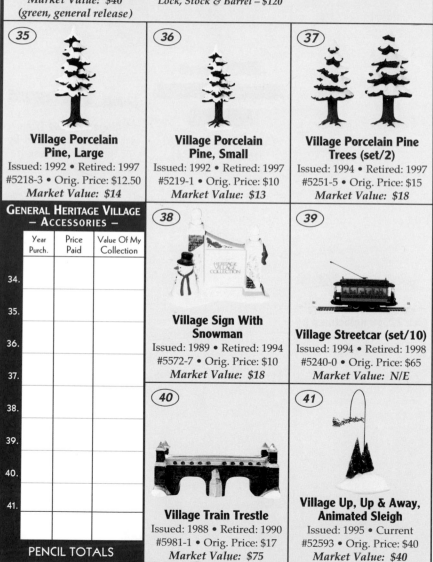

(34)

Village Express Van
Issued: 1992 • Retired: 1996
#5865-3 • Orig. Price: $25
Market Value: $40
(green, general release)

Versions

Black – $140
Gold – $900
Bachman's – $88
Bronner's – $58
The Christmas Dove – $63
European Imports – $56
Fortunoff – $122
Incredible Xmas Place – $73
Lemon Tree – N/E
The Limited Edition – $102
Lock, Stock & Barrel – $120

North Pole City – $62
Parkwest – $515
Robert's – $58
St. Nick's – $65
Stats – $58
William Glen – $62
The Windsor Shoppe – $60

(35)

Village Porcelain Pine, Large
Issued: 1992 • Retired: 1997
#5218-3 • Orig. Price: $12.50
Market Value: $14

(36)

Village Porcelain Pine, Small
Issued: 1992 • Retired: 1997
#5219-1 • Orig. Price: $10
Market Value: $13

(37)

Village Porcelain Pine Trees (set/2)
Issued: 1994 • Retired: 1997
#5251-5 • Orig. Price: $15
Market Value: $18

GENERAL HERITAGE VILLAGE – ACCESSORIES –

	Year Purch.	Price Paid	Value Of My Collection
34.			
35.			
36.			
37.			
38.			
39.			
40.			
41.			
PENCIL TOTALS			

(38)

Village Sign With Snowman
Issued: 1989 • Retired: 1994
#5572-7 • Orig. Price: $10
Market Value: $18

(39)

Village Streetcar (set/10)
Issued: 1994 • Retired: 1998
#5240-0 • Orig. Price: $65
Market Value: N/E

(40)

Village Train Trestle
Issued: 1988 • Retired: 1990
#5981-1 • Orig. Price: $17
Market Value: $75

(41)

Village Up, Up & Away, Animated Sleigh
Issued: 1995 • Current
#52593 • Orig. Price: $40
Market Value: $40

(42)

Village Waterfall
Issued: 1996 • Current
#52644 • Orig. Price: $65
Market Value: $40

DICKENS' VILLAGE ACCESSORIES

The first of the *Dickens' Village* accessories were issued in 1984. This year, seven new accessories join *Dickens' Village*, bringing the total number for the village to 88.

GENERAL/DICKENS' VILLAGE — ACCESSORIES —

(1) New!

Ale Mates (set/2)
Issued: 1998 • Current
#58417 • Orig. Price: $25
Market Value: $25

(2) ✓

Ashley Pond Skating Party (set/6)
Issued: 1997 • Current
#58405 • Orig. Price: $70
Market Value: $70

(3)

The Bird Seller (set/3)
Issued: 1992 • Retired: 1995
#5803-3 • Orig. Price: $25
Market Value: $37

(4)

Blacksmith (set/3)
Issued: 1987 • Retired: 1990
#5934-0 • Orig. Price: $20
Market Value: $85

(5) ✓

Bringing Fleeces To The Mill (set/2)
Issued: 1993 • Retired: 1998
#5819-0 • Orig. Price: $35
Market Value: $38

(6) ✓

Bringing Home The Yule Log (set/3)
Issued: 1991 • Retired: 1998
#5558-1 • Orig. Price: $27.50
Market Value: $30

(7)

Brixton Road Watchman (set/2)
Issued: 1995 • Current
#58390 • Orig. Price: $25
Market Value: $25

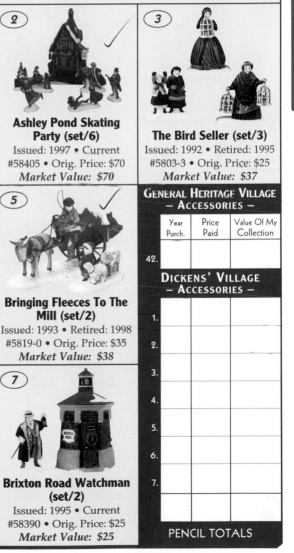

GENERAL HERITAGE VILLAGE — ACCESSORIES —

	Year Purch.	Price Paid	Value Of My Collection
42.			

DICKENS' VILLAGE — ACCESSORIES —

1.			
2.			
3.			
4.			
5.			
6.			
7.			
PENCIL TOTALS			

8

C. Bradford, Wheelwright & Son (set/2)
Issued: 1993 • Retired: 1996
#5818-1 • Orig. Price: $24
Market Value: $31

9

Version 1   Version 2   Version 3

Carolers (set/3)
Issued: 1984 • Retired: 1990
#6526-9 • Orig. Price: $10
Market Value: 1 – $115 (white lamppost)
2 – $39 (black lamppost, tan viola)
3 – N/E (black lamppost, brown/tan viola)

10

Carolers On The Doorstep (set/4)
Issued: 1990 • Retired: 1993
#5570-0 • Orig. Price: $25
Market Value: $44

11

Caroling With The Cratchit Family (set/3)
Christmas Carol Revisited
Issued: 1996 • Current
#58396 • Orig. Price: $37.50
Market Value: $37.50

12

Chelsea Lane Shoppers (set/4)
Issued: 1993 • Current
#5816-5 • Orig. Price: $30
Market Value: $30

DICKENS' VILLAGE
– ACCESSORIES –

	Year Purch.	Price Paid	Value Of My Collection
8.			
9.			
10.			
11.			
12.			
13.			
14.			
15.			
16.			
PENCIL TOTALS			

13

Chelsea Market Curiosities Monger & Cart (set/2)
Issued: 1994 • Retired: 1998
#5827-0 • Orig. Price: $27.50
Market Value: $30

14

Chelsea Market Fish Monger & Cart (set/2)
Issued: 1993 • Retired: 1997
#5814-9 • Orig. Price: $25
Market Value: $31

15

Chelsea Market Flower Monger & Cart (set/2)
Issued: 1993 • Current
#5815-7 • Orig. Price: $27.50
Market Value: $27.50

16

Chelsea Market Fruit Monger & Cart (set/2)
Issued: 1993 • Retired: 1997
#5813-0 • Orig. Price: $25
Market Value: $33

17 ✓

Chelsea Market Hat Monger & Cart (set/2)
Issued: 1995 • Current
#58392 • Orig. Price: $27.50
Market Value: $27.50

18 ✓

Chelsea Market Mistletoe Monger & Cart (set/2)
Issued: 1994 • Retired: 1998
#5826-2 • Orig. Price: $25
Market Value: $27

19 New!

Child's Play (set/2)
Issued: 1998 • Current
#58415 • Orig. Price: $25
Market Value: $25

20

Childe Pond & Skaters (set/4)
Issued: 1988 • Retired: 1991
#5903-0 • Orig. Price: $30
Market Value: $87

21 ✓

Christmas Carol Christmas Morning Figures (set/3)
Issued: 1989 • Current
#5588-3 • Orig. Price: $18
Market Value: $18

22

Christmas Carol Christmas Spirits Figures (set/4)
Issued: 1989 • Current
#5589-1 • Orig. Price: $27.50
Market Value: $27.50

23

Christmas Carol Figures (set/3)
Issued: 1986 • Retired: 1990
#6501-3 • Orig. Price: $12.50
Market Value: $85

24

Christmas Carol Holiday Trimming Set (set/21)
Issued: 1994 • Retired: 1997
#5831-9 • Orig. Price: $65
Market Value: $75

25

"A Christmas Carol" Reading By Charles Dickens (set/4)
Issued: 1996 • Current
#58403 • Orig. Price: $45
Market Value: $45

DICKENS' VILLAGE – ACCESSORIES –

	Year Purch.	Price Paid	Value Of My Collection
17.			
18.			
19.			
20.			
21.			
22.			
23.			
24.			
25.			
PENCIL TOTALS			

DICKENS' VILLAGE – ACCESSORIES –

26 "A Christmas Carol" Reading By Charles Dickens (set/7, LE-42,500)
Charles Dickens' Signature Series
Issued: 1996 • Retired: 1997
#58404 • Orig. Price: $75
Market Value: $152

27 Christmas Pudding Costermonger (set/3)
Issued: 1997 • Current
#58408 • Orig. Price: $32.50
Market Value: $32.50

28 Cobbler & Clock Peddler (set/2)
Issued: 1995 • Retired: 1997
#58394 • Orig. Price: $25
Market Value: $29

29 Come Into The Inn (set/3)
Issued: 1991 • Retired: 1994
#5560-3 • Orig. Price: $22
Market Value: $38

30 Constables (set/3)
Issued: 1989 • Retired: 1991
#5579-4 • Orig. Price: $17.50
Market Value: $68

31 David Copperfield Characters (set/5)
Issued: 1989 • Retired: 1992
#5551-4 • Orig. Price: $32.50
Market Value: $48

DICKENS' VILLAGE – ACCESSORIES –

	Year Purch.	Price Paid	Value Of My Collection
26.			
27.			
28.			
29.			
30.			
31.			
32.			
33.			
PENCIL TOTALS			

32 Delivering Coal For The Hearth (set/2)
Issued: 1997 • Current
#58326 • Orig. Price: $32.50
Market Value: $32.50

33 Dickens' Village Sign
Issued: 1987 • Retired: 1993
#6569-2 • Orig. Price: $6
Market Value: $20

(34)

Version 1   Version 2   Version 3

Dover Coach
Issued: 1987 • Retired: 1990
#6590-0 • Orig. Price: $18
Market Value: **1** – *$100 (without mustache)*
2 – *$73 (with mustache, tight reins)*
3 – *N/E (with mustache, loose reins)*

(35)

Eight Maids A-Milking
(set/2)
The Twelve Days Of
Dickens' Village
Issued: 1996 • Current
#58384 • Orig. Price: $25
Market Value: $25

(36) New!

Eleven Lords A-Leaping
The Twelve Days Of
Dickens' Village
Issued: 1998 • Current
#58413 • Orig. Price: $27.50
Market Value: $27.50

(37)

English Post Box
Issued: 1992 • Current
#58050 • Orig. Price: $4.50
Market Value: $4.50

(38)

Farm People & Animals
(set/5)
Issued: 1987 • Retired: 1989
#5901-3 • Orig. Price: $24
Market Value: $99

(39)

Version 1   Version 2

Father Christmas's Journey (track compatible)
Issued: 1997 • Current
#58407 • Orig. Price: $30
Market Value: **1** – *$30 (general release)*
2 – *N/E (North Pole City)*

(40)

Fezziwig And Friends
(set/3)
Issued: 1988 • Retired: 1990
#5928-5 • Orig. Price: $12.50
Market Value: $57

DICKENS' VILLAGE — ACCESSORIES —

DICKENS' VILLAGE
– ACCESSORIES –

	Year Purch.	Price Paid	Value Of My Collection
34.			
35.			
36.			
37.			
38.			
39.			
40.			

PENCIL TOTALS

(41) Version 1   Version 2

The Fezziwig Delivery Wagon
Christmas Carol Revisited
Issued: 1996 • Current
#58400 • Orig. Price: $32.50
Market Value:
1 – $32.50 (general release) 2 – N/E (Lord & Taylor)

(42)

The Fire Brigade Of London Town (set/5)
Issued: 1997 • Current
#58406 • Orig. Price: $70
Market Value: $70

(43)

Five Golden Rings (set/2)
The Twelve Days Of Dickens' Village
Issued: 1995 • Current
#58381 • Orig. Price: $27.50
Market Value: $27.50

(44)

The Flying Scot Train (set/4)
Issued: 1990 • Retired: 1998
#5573-5 • Orig. Price: $48
Market Value: $56

(45)

Four Calling Birds
The Twelve Days Of Dickens' Village
Issued: 1995 • Current
#58379 • Orig. Price: $32.50
Market Value: $32.50

DICKENS' VILLAGE
– ACCESSORIES –

	Year Purch.	Price Paid	Value Of My Collection
41.			
42.			
43.			
44.			
45.			
46.			
47.			
48.			
PENCIL TOTALS			

(46)

Gingerbread Vendor (set/2)
Issued: 1996 • Current
#58402 • Orig. Price: $22.50
Market Value: $22.50

(47) New!

Here We Come A-Wassailing (set/5)
Issued: 1998 • Current
#58410 • Orig. Price: $45
Market Value: $45

(48)

Holiday Coach
Issued: 1991 • Retired: 1998
#5561-1 • Orig. Price: $68
Market Value: $75

49

50

51

Holiday Travelers (set/3)
Issued: 1990 • Current
#5571-9 • Orig. Price: $22.50
Market Value: $25

King's Road Cab
Issued: 1989 • Retired: 1998
#5581-6 • Orig. Price: $30
Market Value: $35

Lamplighter w/Lamp (set/2)
Issued: 1989 • Current
#5577-8 • Orig. Price: $9
Market Value: $10

52

53

54

Nine Ladies Dancing (set/2)
The Twelve Days Of Dickens' Village
Issued: 1997 • Current
#58385 • Orig. Price: $30
Market Value: $30

Lionhead Bridge
Issued: 1992 • Retired: 1997
#5864-5 • Orig. Price: $22
Market Value: $30

Nicholas Nickleby Characters (set/4)
Issued: 1988 • Retired: 1991
#5929-3 • Orig. Price: $20
Market Value: $43

55

56

The Old Puppeteer (set/3)
Issued: 1992 • Retired: 1995
#5802-5 • Orig. Price: $32
Market Value: $43

Oliver Twist Characters (set/3)
Issued: 1991 • Retired: 1993
#5554-9 • Orig. Price: $35
Market Value: $49

57 *Version 1* *Version 2*

Ox Sled
Issued: 1987 • Retired: 1989
#5951-0 • Orig. Price: $20
Market Value: 1 – $260 (tan pants/green seat)
2 – $145 (blue pants/black seat)

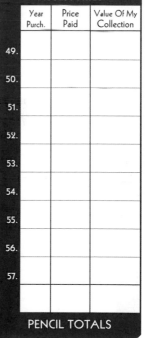

DICKENS' VILLAGE
– ACCESSORIES –

	Year Purch.	Price Paid	Value Of My Collection
49.			
50.			
51.			
52.			
53.			
54.			
55.			
56.			
57.			

PENCIL TOTALS

58

A Partridge In A Pear Tree
The Twelve Days Of Dickens' Village
Issued: 1995 • Current
#5835-1 • Orig. Price: $35
Market Value: $35

59

A Peaceful Glow On Christmas Eve (set/3)
Issued: 1994 • Current
#5830-0 • Orig. Price: $30
Market Value: $30

60

Portobello Road Peddlers (set/3)
Issued: 1994 • Retired: 1998
#5828-9 • Orig. Price: $27.50
Market Value: $30

61

Postern (Dickens' Village Ten Year Anniversary Piece)
Issued: 1994 • Retired: 1994
#9871-0 • Orig. Price: $17.50
Market Value: $34

62

Poultry Market (set/3)
Issued: 1991 • Retired: 1995
#5559-0 • Orig. Price: $30
Market Value: $46

63

Red Christmas Sulky
Issued: 1996 • Current
#58401 • Orig. Price: $30
Market Value: $30

DICKENS' VILLAGE – ACCESSORIES –		
Year Purch.	Price Paid	Value Of My Collection
58.		
59.		
60.		
61.		
62.		
63.		
64.		
65.		
66.		
67.		
PENCIL TOTALS		

64

Royal Coach
Issued: 1989 • Retired: 1992
#5578-6 • Orig. Price: $55
Market Value: $85

65

Seven Swans A-Swimming (set/4)
The Twelve Days Of Dickens' Village
Issued: 1996 • Current
#58383 • Orig. Price: $27.50
Market Value: $27.50

66

Shopkeepers (set/4)
Issued: 1987 • Retired: 1988
#5966-8 • Orig. Price: $15
Market Value: $42

67

Silo & Hay Shed (set/2)
Issued: 1987 • Retired: 1989
#5950-1 • Orig. Price: $18
Market Value: $170

68 New!

Sitting In Camden Park (set/4)
Issued: 1998 • Current
#58411 • Orig. Price: $35
Market Value: $35

69

Six Geese A-Laying (set/2)
The Twelve Days Of Dickens' Village
Issued: 1995 • Current
#58382 • Orig. Price: $30
Market Value: $30

70

Stone Bridge
Issued: 1987 • Retired: 1990
#6546-3 • Orig. Price: $12
Market Value: $82

71

"Tallyho!" (set/5)
Issued: 1995 • Retired: 1998
#58391 • Orig. Price: $50
Market Value: $52

72

Ten Pipers Piping (set/3)
The Twelve Days Of Dickens' Village
Issued: 1997 • Current
#58386 • Orig. Price: $30
Market Value: $30

73 New!

Tending The Cold Frame (set/3)
Issued: 1998 • Current
#58416 • Orig. Price: $32.50
Market Value: $32.50

74

Tending The New Calves (set/3)
Issued: 1996 • Current
#58395 • Orig. Price: $30
Market Value: $30

75

Thatchers (set/3)
Issued: 1994 • Retired: 1997
#5829-7 • Orig. Price: $35
Market Value: $38

76

Three French Hens (set/3)
The Twelve Days Of Dickens' Village
Issued: 1995 • Current
#58378 • Orig. Price: $32.50
Market Value: $32.50

77

Town Crier & Chimney Sweep (set/2)
Issued: 1990 • Current
#5569-7 • Orig. Price: $15
Market Value: $16

DICKENS' VILLAGE – ACCESSORIES –

	Year Purch.	Price Paid	Value Of My Collection
68.			
69.			
70.			
71.			
72.			
73.			
74.			
75.			
76.			
77.			
PENCIL TOTALS			

DICKENS' VILLAGE – ACCESSORIES –

95

78

Two Turtle Doves (set/4)
*The Twelve Days Of
Dickens' Village*
Issued: 1995 • Current
#5836-0 • Orig. Price: $32.50
Market Value: $32.50

79 New!

**Until We Meet Again
(set/2)**
Issued: 1998 • Current
#58414 • Orig. Price: $27.50
Market Value: $27.50

80

**Victoria Station Train
Platform**
Issued: 1990 • Current
#5575-1 • Orig. Price: $20
Market Value: $22

81

**Village Street Peddlers
(set/2)**
Issued: 1992 • Retired: 1994
#5804-1 • Orig. Price: $16
Market Value: $32

82

Village Train (set/3)
Issued: 1985 • Retired: 1986
#6527-7 • Orig. Price: $12
Market Value: $430

83

**Village Well & Holy Cross
(set/2)**
Issued: 1987 • Retired: 1989
#6547-1 • Orig. Price: $13
Market Value: $154

**DICKENS' VILLAGE
– ACCESSORIES –**

	Year Purch.	Price Paid	Value Of My Collection
78.			
79.			
80.			
81.			
82.			
83.			
84.			
85.			
86.			
87.			
PENCIL TOTALS			

84

**Violet Vendor/Carolers/
Chestnut Vendor (set/3)**
Issued: 1989 • Retired: 1992
#5580-8 • Orig. Price: $23
Market Value: $45

85

**Vision Of A Christmas
Past (set/3)**
Issued: 1993 • Retired: 1996
#5817-3 • Orig. Price: $27.50
Market Value: $37

86

Winter Sleighride
Issued: 1994 • Current
#5825-4 • Orig. Price: $18
Market Value: $18

87

**"Ye Olde Lamplighter"
Dickens' Village Sign**
Issued: 1995 • Current
#58393 • Orig. Price: $20
Market Value: $20

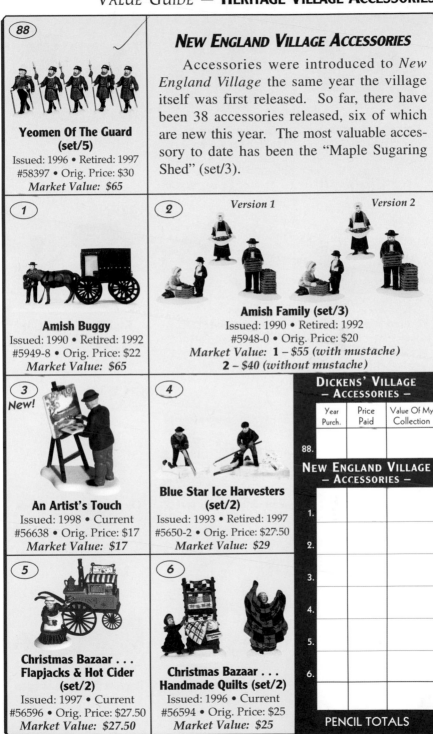

88

Yeomen Of The Guard (set/5)
Issued: 1996 • Retired: 1997
#58397 • Orig. Price: $30
Market Value: $65

NEW ENGLAND VILLAGE ACCESSORIES

Accessories were introduced to *New England Village* the same year the village itself was first released. So far, there have been 38 accessories released, six of which are new this year. The most valuable accessory to date has been the "Maple Sugaring Shed" (set/3).

1

Amish Buggy
Issued: 1990 • Retired: 1992
#5949-8 • Orig. Price: $22
Market Value: $65

2

Version 1   Version 2

Amish Family (set/3)
Issued: 1990 • Retired: 1992
#5948-0 • Orig. Price: $20
Market Value: **1** *– $55 (with mustache)*
2 *– $40 (without mustache)*

3 New!

An Artist's Touch
Issued: 1998 • Current
#56638 • Orig. Price: $17
Market Value: $17

4

Blue Star Ice Harvesters (set/2)
Issued: 1993 • Retired: 1997
#5650-2 • Orig. Price: $27.50
Market Value: $29

5

Christmas Bazaar . . . Flapjacks & Hot Cider (set/2)
Issued: 1997 • Current
#56596 • Orig. Price: $27.50
Market Value: $27.50

6

Christmas Bazaar . . . Handmade Quilts (set/2)
Issued: 1996 • Current
#56594 • Orig. Price: $25
Market Value: $25

DICKENS' VILLAGE – ACCESSORIES –

	Year Purch.	Price Paid	Value Of My Collection
88.			

NEW ENGLAND VILLAGE – ACCESSORIES –

1.			
2.			
3.			
4.			
5.			
6.			
PENCIL TOTALS			

DICKENS'/NEW ENGLAND – ACCESSORIES –

(7)

Christmas Bazaar . . . Sign (set/2)
Issued: 1997 • Current
#56598 • Orig. Price: $16
Market Value: $16

(8)

Christmas Bazaar . . . Toy Vendor & Cart (set/2)
Issued: 1997 • Current
#56597 • Orig. Price: $27.50
Market Value: $27.50

(9)

Christmas Bazaar . . . Woolens & Preserves (set/2)
Issued: 1996 • Current
#56595 • Orig. Price: $25
Market Value: $25

(10)

Covered Wooden Bridge
Issued: 1986 • Retired: 1990
#6531-5 • Orig. Price: $10
Market Value: $43

(11)

Farm Animals (set/4)
Issued: 1989 • Retired: 1991
#5945-5 • Orig. Price: $15
Market Value: $45

(12)

Farm Animals (set/8)
Issued: 1995 • Current
#56588 • Orig. Price: $32.50
Market Value: $32.50

NEW ENGLAND VILLAGE – ACCESSORIES –

	Year Purch.	Price Paid	Value Of My Collection
7.			
8.			
9.			
10.			
11.			
12.			
13.			
14.			
15.			
16.			
PENCIL TOTALS			

(13)
New!

Farmer's Market (set/2)
Issued: 1998 • Current
#56637 • Orig. Price: $55
Market Value: $55

(14)
New!

Fly-casting In The Brook
Issued: 1998 • Current
#56633 • Orig. Price: $15
Market Value: $15

(15)

"Fresh Paint" New England Village Sign
Issued: 1995 • Current
#56592 • Orig. Price: $20
Market Value: $20

(16)

Harvest Pumpkin Wagon
Issued: 1995 • Current
#56591 • Orig. Price: $45
Market Value: $45

(17)

(18)

(19)
New!

Harvest Seed Cart (set/3)
Issued: 1992 • Retired: 1995
#5645-6 • Orig. Price: $27.50
Market Value: $42

Knife Grinder (set/2)
Issued: 1993 • Retired: 1996
#5649-9 • Orig. Price: $22.50
Market Value: $30

Load Up The Wagon (set/2)
Issued: 1998 • Current
#56630 • Orig. Price: $40
Market Value: $40

(20)

(21)

(22)

Lobster Trappers (set/4)
Issued: 1995 • Current
#56589 • Orig. Price: $35
Market Value: $35

Lumberjacks (set/2)
Issued: 1995 • Retired: 1998
#56590 • Orig. Price: $30
Market Value: $34

Maple Sugaring Shed (set/3)
Issued: 1987 • Retired: 1989
#6589-7 • Orig. Price: $19
Market Value: $255

(23)

(24)

Market Day (set/3)
Issued: 1991 • Retired: 1993
#5641-3 • Orig. Price: $35
Market Value: $49

New England Village Sign
Issued: 1987 • Retired: 1993
#6570-6 • Orig. Price: $6
Market Value: $21

(25)

New England Winter Set (set/5)
Issued: 1986 • Retired: 1990
#6532-3 • Orig. Price: $18
Market Value: $50

NEW ENGLAND VILLAGE
– ACCESSORIES –

	Year Purch.	Price Paid	Value Of My Collection
17.			
18.			
19.			
20.			
21.			
22.			
23.			
24.			
25.			
PENCIL TOTALS			

NEW ENGLAND VILLAGE – ACCESSORIES –

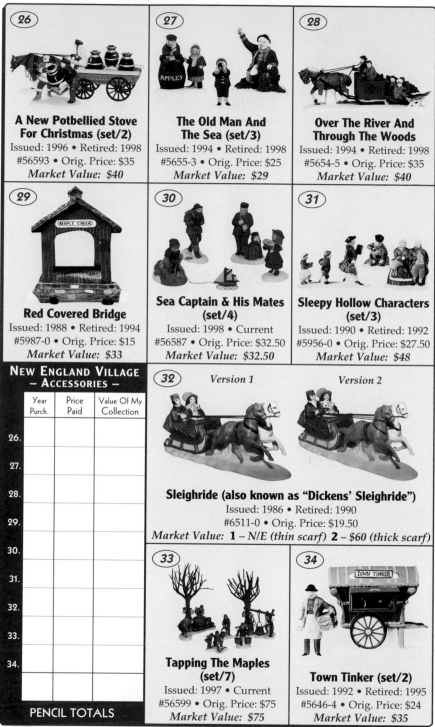

26

A New Potbellied Stove For Christmas (set/2)
Issued: 1996 • Retired: 1998
#56593 • Orig. Price: $35
Market Value: $40

27

The Old Man And The Sea (set/3)
Issued: 1994 • Retired: 1998
#5655-3 • Orig. Price: $25
Market Value: $29

28

Over The River And Through The Woods
Issued: 1994 • Retired: 1998
#5654-5 • Orig. Price: $35
Market Value: $40

29

Red Covered Bridge
Issued: 1988 • Retired: 1994
#5987-0 • Orig. Price: $15
Market Value: $33

30

Sea Captain & His Mates (set/4)
Issued: 1998 • Current
#56587 • Orig. Price: $32.50
Market Value: $32.50

31

Sleepy Hollow Characters (set/3)
Issued: 1990 • Retired: 1992
#5956-0 • Orig. Price: $27.50
Market Value: $48

NEW ENGLAND VILLAGE – ACCESSORIES –

	Year Purch.	Price Paid	Value Of My Collection
26.			
27.			
28.			
29.			
30.			
31.			
32.			
33.			
34.			
PENCIL TOTALS			

32   Version 1   Version 2

Sleighride (also known as "Dickens' Sleighride")
Issued: 1986 • Retired: 1990
#6511-0 • Orig. Price: $19.50
*Market Value: **1** – N/E (thin scarf) **2** – $60 (thick scarf)*

33

Tapping The Maples (set/7)
Issued: 1997 • Current
#56599 • Orig. Price: $75
Market Value: $75

34

Town Tinker (set/2)
Issued: 1992 • Retired: 1995
#5646-4 • Orig. Price: $24
Market Value: $35

35
New!

Under The Mistletoe
Issued: 1998 • Current
#56631 • Orig. Price: $16.50
Market Value: $16.50

36

**Village Harvest People
(set/4)**
Issued: 1988 • Retired: 1991
#5941-2 • Orig. Price: $27.50
Market Value: $55

37
New!

**Volunteer Firefighters
(set/2)**
Issued: 1998 • Current
#56635 • Orig. Price: $37.50
Market Value: $37.50

38

**Woodcutter And
Son (set/2)**
Issued: 1988 • Retired: 1990
#5986-2 • Orig. Price: $10
Market Value: $50

ALPINE VILLAGE ACCESSORIES

Only two new accessories join *Alpine Village* for 1999, bringing the total number to a lucky 13. A unique piece in this village's accessory selection is "Silent Night," which is a musical. The most valuable piece on the secondary market is "Alpine Villagers" (set/3).

1

**"Alpen Horn Player"
Alpine Village Sign**
Issued: 1995 • Current
#56182 • Orig. Price: $20
Market Value: $20

2

Alpine Village Sign
Issued: 1987 • Retired: 1993
#6571-4 • Orig. Price: $6
Market Value: $20

3

Alpine Villagers (set/3)
Issued: 1986 • Retired: 1992
#6542-0 • Orig. Price: $13
Market Value: $38

4

**Buying Bakers Bread
(set/2)**
Issued: 1992 • Retired: 1995
#5619-7 • Orig. Price: $20
Market Value: $37

NEW ENGLAND/ALPINE – ACCESSORIES –

NEW ENGLAND VILLAGE – ACCESSORIES –

	Year Purch.	Price Paid	Value Of My Collection
35.			
36.			
37.			
38.			

ALPINE VILLAGE – ACCESSORIES –

1.			
2.			
3.			
4.			

PENCIL TOTALS

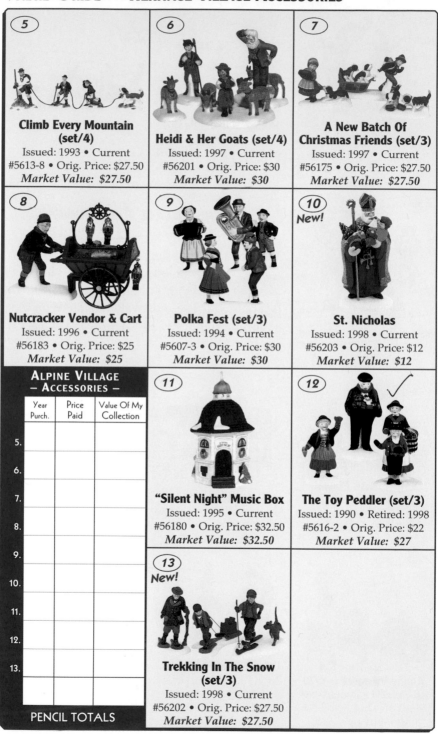

5

Climb Every Mountain (set/4)
Issued: 1993 • Current
#5613-8 • Orig. Price: $27.50
Market Value: $27.50

6

Heidi & Her Goats (set/4)
Issued: 1997 • Current
#56201 • Orig. Price: $30
Market Value: $30

7

A New Batch Of Christmas Friends (set/3)
Issued: 1997 • Current
#56175 • Orig. Price: $27.50
Market Value: $27.50

8

Nutcracker Vendor & Cart
Issued: 1996 • Current
#56183 • Orig. Price: $25
Market Value: $25

9

Polka Fest (set/3)
Issued: 1994 • Current
#5607-3 • Orig. Price: $30
Market Value: $30

10
New!

St. Nicholas
Issued: 1998 • Current
#56203 • Orig. Price: $12
Market Value: $12

ALPINE VILLAGE — ACCESSORIES —

	Year Purch.	Price Paid	Value Of My Collection
5.			
6.			
7.			
8.			
9.			
10.			
11.			
12.			
13.			
PENCIL TOTALS			

11

"Silent Night" Music Box
Issued: 1995 • Current
#56180 • Orig. Price: $32.50
Market Value: $32.50

12

The Toy Peddler (set/3)
Issued: 1990 • Retired: 1998
#5616-2 • Orig. Price: $22
Market Value: $27

13
New!

Trekking In The Snow (set/3)
Issued: 1998 • Current
#56202 • Orig. Price: $27.50
Market Value: $27.50

CHRISTMAS IN THE CITY ACCESSORIES

Of the 44 accessories that are part of *Christmas in the City*, 17 are still current. The first of the accessories were introduced in 1987 and have produced several valuable pieces. The most valuable to date has been the "Salvation Army Band" (set/6).

1 New!

1919 Ford® Model-T
Issued: 1998 • Current
#58906 • Orig. Price: $20
Market Value: $20

2

All Around The Town (set/2)
Issued: 1991 • Retired: 1993
#5545-0 • Orig. Price: $18
Market Value: $32

3

Automobiles (set/3)
Issued: 1987 • Retired: 1996
#5964-1 • Orig. Price: $15
Market Value: $28

4

Big Smile For The Camera (set/2)
Issued: 1997 • Current
#58900 • Orig. Price: $27.50
Market Value: $27.50

5

Boulevard (set/14)
Issued: 1989 • Retired: 1992
#5516-6 • Orig. Price: $25
Market Value: $56

6

Busy Sidewalks (set/4)
Issued: 1990 • Retired: 1992
#5535-2 • Orig. Price: $28
Market Value: $52

7

Caroling Thru The City (set/3)
Issued: 1991 • Retired: 1998
#5548-4 • Orig. Price: $27.50
Market Value: $31

8 New!

A Carriage Ride For The Bride (track compatible)
Issued: 1998 • Current
#58901 • Orig. Price: $40
Market Value: $40

CHRISTMAS IN THE CITY
– ACCESSORIES –

	Year Purch.	Price Paid	Value Of My Collection
1.			
2.			
3.			
4.			
5.			
6.			
7.			
8.			
PENCIL TOTALS			

CHRISTMAS IN THE CITY – ACCESSORIES –

103

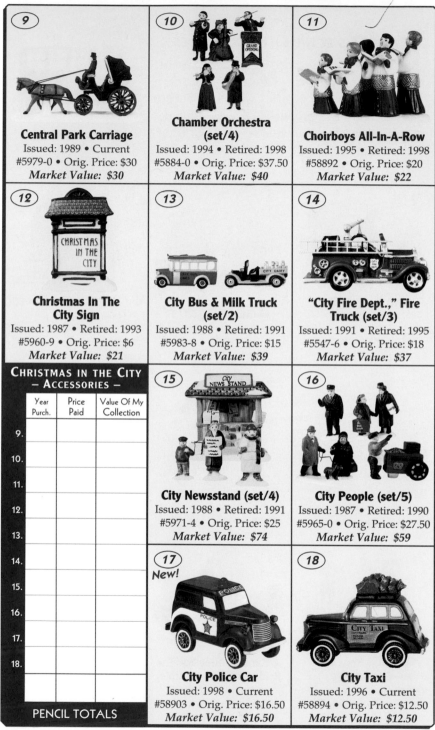

9

Central Park Carriage
Issued: 1989 • Current
#5979-0 • Orig. Price: $30
Market Value: $30

10

Chamber Orchestra (set/4)
Issued: 1994 • Retired: 1998
#5884-0 • Orig. Price: $37.50
Market Value: $40

11

Choirboys All-In-A-Row
Issued: 1995 • Retired: 1998
#58892 • Orig. Price: $20
Market Value: $22

12

Christmas In The City Sign
Issued: 1987 • Retired: 1993
#5960-9 • Orig. Price: $6
Market Value: $21

13

City Bus & Milk Truck (set/2)
Issued: 1988 • Retired: 1991
#5983-8 • Orig. Price: $15
Market Value: $39

14

"City Fire Dept.," Fire Truck (set/3)
Issued: 1991 • Retired: 1995
#5547-6 • Orig. Price: $18
Market Value: $37

CHRISTMAS IN THE CITY – ACCESSORIES –

	Year Purch.	Price Paid	Value Of My Collection
9.			
10.			
11.			
12.			
13.			
14.			
15.			
16.			
17.			
18.			
PENCIL TOTALS			

15

City Newsstand (set/4)
Issued: 1988 • Retired: 1991
#5971-4 • Orig. Price: $25
Market Value: $74

16

City People (set/5)
Issued: 1987 • Retired: 1990
#5965-0 • Orig. Price: $27.50
Market Value: $59

17
New!

City Police Car
Issued: 1998 • Current
#58903 • Orig. Price: $16.50
Market Value: $16.50

18

City Taxi
Issued: 1996 • Current
#58894 • Orig. Price: $12.50
Market Value: $12.50

19

City Workers (set/4)
Issued: 1987 • Retired: 1988
#5967-6 • Orig. Price: $15
Market Value: $45

20

Don't Drop The Presents! (set/2)
Issued: 1992 • Retired: 1995
#5532-8 • Orig. Price: $25
Market Value: $37

21

The Family Tree
Issued: 1996 • Current
#58895 • Orig. Price: $18
Market Value: $18

22

The Fire Brigade (set/2)
Issued: 1991 • Retired: 1995
#5546-8 • Orig. Price: $20
Market Value: $35

23

Going Home For The Holidays (set/3)
Issued: 1996 • Current
#58896 • Orig. Price: $27.50
Market Value: $27.50

24 ✓

Holiday Field Trip (set/3)
Issued: 1994 • Retired: 1998
#5885-8 • Orig. Price: $27.50
Market Value: $30

25

Hot Dog Vendor (set/3)
Issued: 1994 • Retired: 1997
#5886-6 • Orig. Price: $27.50
Market Value: $31

26

Johnson's Grocery . . . Holiday Deliveries (track compatible)
Issued: 1997 • Current
#58897 • Orig. Price: $18
Market Value: $18

27

"A Key To The City" Christmas In The City Sign
Issued: 1995 • Current
#58893 • Orig. Price: $20
Market Value: $20

28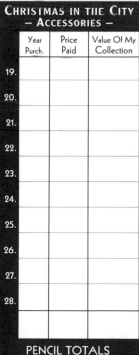

Let's Go Shopping In The City (set/3)
Issued: 1997 • Current
#58899 • Orig. Price: $35
Market Value: $35

CHRISTMAS IN THE CITY — ACCESSORIES —

	Year Purch.	Price Paid	Value Of My Collection
19.			
20.			
21.			
22.			
23.			
24.			
25.			
26.			
27.			
28.			
PENCIL TOTALS			

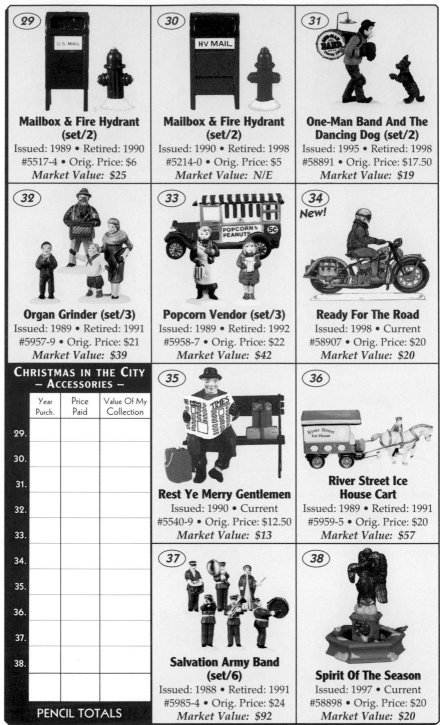

(29)

Mailbox & Fire Hydrant (set/2)
Issued: 1989 • Retired: 1990
#5517-4 • Orig. Price: $6
Market Value: $25

(30)

Mailbox & Fire Hydrant (set/2)
Issued: 1990 • Retired: 1998
#5214-0 • Orig. Price: $5
Market Value: N/E

(31)

One-Man Band And The Dancing Dog (set/2)
Issued: 1995 • Retired: 1998
#58891 • Orig. Price: $17.50
Market Value: $19

(32)

Organ Grinder (set/3)
Issued: 1989 • Retired: 1991
#5957-9 • Orig. Price: $21
Market Value: $39

(33)

Popcorn Vendor (set/3)
Issued: 1989 • Retired: 1992
#5958-7 • Orig. Price: $22
Market Value: $42

(34) New!

Ready For The Road
Issued: 1998 • Current
#58907 • Orig. Price: $20
Market Value: $20

CHRISTMAS IN THE CITY – ACCESSORIES –

	Year Purch.	Price Paid	Value Of My Collection
29.			
30.			
31.			
32.			
33.			
34.			
35.			
36.			
37.			
38.			
PENCIL TOTALS			

(35)

Rest Ye Merry Gentlemen
Issued: 1990 • Current
#5540-9 • Orig. Price: $12.50
Market Value: $13

(36)

River Street Ice House Cart
Issued: 1989 • Retired: 1991
#5959-5 • Orig. Price: $20
Market Value: $57

(37)

Salvation Army Band (set/6)
Issued: 1988 • Retired: 1991
#5985-4 • Orig. Price: $24
Market Value: $92

(38)

Spirit Of The Season
Issued: 1997 • Current
#58898 • Orig. Price: $20
Market Value: $20

Steppin' Out On The Town (set/5)
Issued: 1997 • Current
#58885 • Orig. Price: $35
Market Value: $35

Street Musicians (set/3)
Issued: 1993 • Retired: 1997
#5564-6 • Orig. Price: $25
Market Value: $36

'Tis The Season
Issued: 1990 • Retired: 1994
#5539-5 • Orig. Price: $12.50
Market Value: $26

42 New!

To Protect And To Serve (set/3)
Issued: 1998 • Current
#58902 • Orig. Price: $32.50
Market Value: $32.50

Welcome Home (set/3)
Issued: 1992 • Retired: 1995
#5533-6 • Orig. Price: $27.50
Market Value: $37

"Yes, Virginia . . ." (set/2)
Issued: 1995 • Current
#58890 • Orig. Price: $12.50
Market Value: $12.50

NORTH POLE ACCESSORIES

North Pole has the most accessories released this year of any collection in Heritage Village. With the eight new additions for 1999, there are now a total of 34 accessories to complement the village Santa calls home.

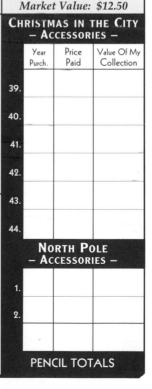

1

Baker Elves (set/3)
Issued: 1991 • Retired: 1995
#5603-0 • Orig. Price: $27.50
Market Value: $45

2

"A Busy Elf" North Pole Sign
Issued: 1995 • Current
#56366 • Orig. Price: $20
Market Value: $20

CHRISTMAS IN THE CITY — ACCESSORIES —		
Year Purch.	Price Paid	Value Of My Collection
39.		
40.		
41.		
42.		
43.		
44.		
NORTH POLE — ACCESSORIES —		
1.		
2.		
PENCIL TOTALS		

(side tab) **CHRISTMAS/NORTH POLE — ACCESSORIES —**

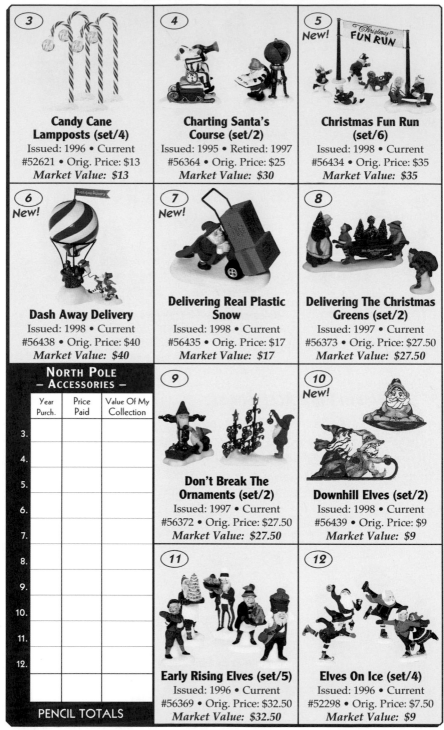

3

Candy Cane Lampposts (set/4)
Issued: 1996 • Current
#52621 • Orig. Price: $13
Market Value: $13

4

Charting Santa's Course (set/2)
Issued: 1995 • Retired: 1997
#56364 • Orig. Price: $25
Market Value: $30

5 New! Christmas FUN RUN

Christmas Fun Run (set/6)
Issued: 1998 • Current
#56434 • Orig. Price: $35
Market Value: $35

6 New!

Dash Away Delivery
Issued: 1998 • Current
#56438 • Orig. Price: $40
Market Value: $40

7 New!

Delivering Real Plastic Snow
Issued: 1998 • Current
#56435 • Orig. Price: $17
Market Value: $17

8

Delivering The Christmas Greens (set/2)
Issued: 1997 • Current
#56373 • Orig. Price: $27.50
Market Value: $27.50

NORTH POLE
– ACCESSORIES –

	Year Purch.	Price Paid	Value Of My Collection
3.			
4.			
5.			
6.			
7.			
8.			
9.			
10.			
11.			
12.			
PENCIL TOTALS			

9

Don't Break The Ornaments (set/2)
Issued: 1997 • Current
#56372 • Orig. Price: $27.50
Market Value: $27.50

10 New!

Downhill Elves (set/2)
Issued: 1998 • Current
#56439 • Orig. Price: $9
Market Value: $9

11

Early Rising Elves (set/5)
Issued: 1996 • Current
#56369 • Orig. Price: $32.50
Market Value: $32.50

12

Elves On Ice (set/4)
Issued: 1996 • Current
#52298 • Orig. Price: $7.50
Market Value: $9

(13)

End Of The Line (set/2)
Issued: 1996 • Current
#56370 • Orig. Price: $28
Market Value: $28

(14) New!

Have A Seat (set/6)
Issued: 1998 • Current
#56437 • Orig. Price: $30
Market Value: $30

(15)

Holiday Deliveries
Issued: 1996 • Current
#56371 • Orig. Price: $16.50
Market Value: $16.50

(16)

I'll Need More Toys (set/2)
Issued: 1995 • Retired: 1998
#56365 • Orig. Price: $25
Market Value: $27

(17)

Last Minute Delivery
Issued: 1994 • Retired: 1998
#5636-7 • Orig. Price: $35
Market Value: $37

(18)

Letters For Santa (set/3)
Issued: 1992 • Retired: 1994
#5604-9 • Orig. Price: $30
Market Value: $63

(19) New!

Loading The Sleigh (set/6)
Issued: 1998 • Current
#52732 • Orig. Price: $125
Market Value: $125

(20)

North Pole Express (set/3)
Issued: 1996 • Current
#56368 • Orig. Price: $37.50
Market Value: $37.50

(21)

North Pole Gate
Issued: 1993 • Retired: 1998
#5632-4 • Orig. Price: $32.50
Market Value: $36

(22)

Peppermint Skating Party (set/6)
Issued: 1998 • Current
#56363 • Orig. Price: $64
Market Value: $64

NORTH POLE
– ACCESSORIES –

	Year Purch.	Price Paid	Value Of My Collection
13.			
14.			
15.			
16.			
17.			
18.			
19.			
20.			
21.			
22.			
PENCIL TOTALS			

NORTH POLE – ACCESSORIES –

23 New!

Reindeer Training Camp (set/2)
Issued: 1998 • Current
#56436 • Orig. Price: $27.50
Market Value: $27.50

24

Santa & Mrs. Claus (set/2)
Issued: 1990 • Current
#5609-0 • Orig. Price: $15
Market Value: $15

25

Santa's Little Helpers (set/3)
Issued: 1990 • Retired: 1993
#5610-3 • Orig. Price: $28
Market Value: $63

26

Sing A Song For Santa (set/3)
Issued: 1993 • Retired: 1998
#5631-6 • Orig. Price: $28
Market Value: $31

27

Sleigh & Eight Tiny Reindeer (set/5)
Issued: 1990 • Current
#5611-1 • Orig. Price: $40
Market Value: $42

28

Snow Cone Elves (set/4)
Issued: 1994 • Retired: 1997
#5637-5 • Orig. Price: $30
Market Value: $34

NORTH POLE
— ACCESSORIES —

	Year Purch.	Price Paid	Value Of My Collection
23.			
24.			
25.			
26.			
27.			
28.			
29.			
30.			
31.			
PENCIL TOTALS			

29

Testing The Toys (set/2)
Issued: 1992 • Current
#5605-7 • Orig. Price: $16.50
Market Value: $16.50

30

Toymaker Elves (set/3)
Issued: 1991 • Retired: 1995
#5602-2 • Orig. Price: $27.50
Market Value: $45

31 NORTH POLE

Trimming The North Pole
Issued: 1990 • Retired: 1993
#5608-1 • Orig. Price: $10
Market Value: $40

32

Untangle The Christmas Lights
Issued: 1997 • Current
#56374 • Orig. Price: $35
Market Value: $35

33
New!

Welcome To Elf Land
Elf Land
Issued: 1998 • Current
#56431 • Orig. Price: $35
Market Value: $35

34

Woodsmen Elves (set/3)
Issued: 1993 • Retired: 1995
#5630-8 • Orig. Price: $30
Market Value: $56

DISNEY PARKS VILLAGE SERIES ACCESSORIES

With only four, *Disney Parks Village Series* has the smallest collection of accessories in any of the villages. Three of the accessories were introduced in 1994, while the last was introduced in 1995. All of the pieces subsequently retired in 1996.

1

Balloon Seller (set/2)
Issued: 1995 • Retired: 1996
#53539 • Orig. Price: $25
Market Value: $54

2

Disney Parks Family (set/3)
Issued: 1994 • Retired: 1996
#5354-6 • Orig. Price: $32.50
Market Value: $40

3

Mickey & Minnie (set/2)
Issued: 1994 • Retired: 1996
#5353-8 • Orig. Price: $22.50
Market Value: $34

4

Olde World Antiques Gate
Issued: 1994 • Retired: 1996
#5355-4 • Orig. Price: $15
Market Value: $22

NORTH POLE/DISNEY – ACCESSORIES –

NORTH POLE – ACCESSORIES –

	Year Purch.	Price Paid	Value Of My Collection
32.			
33.			
34.			

DISNEY PARKS VILLAGE SERIES – ACCESSORIES –

	Year Purch.	Price Paid	Value Of My Collection
1.			
2.			
3.			
4.			

PENCIL TOTALS

111

HERITAGE VILLAGE HINGED BOXES

Department 56 has released nine hinged boxes over the past two years – seven for *Dickens' Village* and two for *North Pole.*

① Bah Humbug
Issued: 1997 • Current
#58430 • Orig. Price: $15
Market Value: $15

② Chimney Sweep
Issued: 1998 • Current
#58434 • Orig. Price: $15
Market Value: $15

③ God Bless Us Every One
Issued: 1997 • Current
#58432 • Orig. Price: $13
Market Value: $13

④ New! Royal Coach
Issued: 1998 • Current
#57501 • Orig. Price: $25
Market Value: $25

⑤ New! Sleighride
Issued: 1998 • Current
#57502 • Orig. Price: $20
Market Value: $20

DICKENS' VILLAGE – HINGED BOXES –

	Year Purch.	Price Paid	Value Of My Collection
1.			
2.			
3.			
4.			
5.			
6.			
7.			

NORTH POLE – HINGED BOXES –

8.			
9.			

PENCIL TOTALS

⑥ The Spirit Of Christmas
Issued: 1997 • Current
#58431 • Orig. Price: $15
Market Value: $15

⑦ Town Crier
Issued: 1998 • Current
#58433 • Orig. Price: $15
Market Value: $15

⑧ New! Caroling Elf
Issued: 1998 • Current
#57506 • Orig. Price: $15
Market Value: $15

⑨ New! Elf On A Sled
Issued: 1998 • Current
#57505 • Orig. Price: $15
Market Value: $15

HERITAGE VILLAGE ORNAMENTS

The 17 new ornaments for 1999 are now lighted and battery-operated. Of the new releases, 7 are re-releases.

1 New!

The Cottage Of Bob Cratchit & Tiny Tim

Fezziwig's Warehouse

Scrooge & Marley Counting House

Christmas Carol Cottages (set/3)
Classic Ornament Series
Issued: 1998 • Current
#98745 • Orig. Price: $50
Market Value: $50

2

Crown & Cricket Inn Ornament (LE-1996)
Issued: 1996 • Retired: 1996
#98730 • Orig. Price: $15
Market Value: $30

3

Dedlock Arms Ornament (LE-1994)
Issued: 1994 • Retired: 1994
#9872-8 • Orig. Price: $12.50
Market Value: $26

4

Dickens' Village Church
Classic Ornament Series
Issued: 1997 • Retired: 1998
#98737 • Orig. Price: $15
Market Value: $17

5 New!

Dickens' Village Church
Classic Ornament Series
Issued: 1998 • Current
#98767 • Orig. Price: $20
Market Value: $20

6

Dickens' Village Mill
Classic Ornament Series
Issued: 1997 • Retired: 1998
#98733 • Orig. Price: $15
Market Value: $17

7 New!

Dickens' Village Mill
Classic Ornament Series
Issued: 1998 • Current
#98766 • Orig. Price: $22.50
Market Value: $22.50

8

Gad's Hill Place Ornament (LE-1997)
Issued: 1997 • Retired: 1997
#98732 • Orig. Price: $15
Market Value: $24

9

The Grapes Inn Ornament (LE-1996)
Issued: 1996 • Retired: 1996
#98729 • Orig. Price: $15
Market Value: $26

DICKENS' VILLAGE – ORNAMENTS –

	Year Purch.	Price Paid	Value Of My Collection
1.			
2.			
3.			
4.			
5.			
6.			
7.			
8.			
9.			
PENCIL TOTALS			

DICKENS' VILLAGE – ORNAMENTS –

10

Old Curiosity Shop
Classic Ornament Series
Issued: 1997 • Retired: 1998
#98738 • Orig. Price: $15
Market Value: $17

11
New!

The Old Curiosity Shop
Classic Ornament Series
Issued: 1998 • Current
#98768 • Orig. Price: $20
Market Value: $20

12

The Pied Bull Inn
Ornament (LE-1996)
Issued: 1996 • Retired: 1996
#98731 • Orig. Price: $15
Market Value: $30

13

Sir John Falstaff Inn
Ornament (LE-1995)
Issued: 1995 • Retired: 1995
#9870-1 • Orig. Price: $15
Market Value: $27

14
New!

Captain's Cottage
Classic Ornament Series
Issued: 1998 • Current
#98756 • Orig. Price: $20
Market Value: $20

15

Craggy Cove Lighthouse
Classic Ornament Series
Issued: 1997 • Retired: 1998
#98739 • Orig. Price: $15
Market Value: $17

16
New!

Craggy Cove Lighthouse
Classic Ornament Series
Issued: 1998 • Current
#98769 • Orig. Price: $20
Market Value: $20

17
New!

Steeple Church
Classic Ornament Series
Issued: 1998 • Current
#98757 • Orig. Price: $20
Market Value: $20

18
New!

Cathedral Church Of
St. Mark
Classic Ornament Series
Issued: 1998 • Current
#98759 • Orig. Price: $22.50
Market Value: $22.50

19

City Hall
Classic Ornament Series
Issued: 1997 • Retired: 1998
#98741 • Orig. Price: $15
Market Value: $17

DICKENS' VILLAGE – ORNAMENTS –

	Year Purch.	Price Paid	Value Of My Collection
10.			
11.			
12.			
13.			

NEW ENGLAND VILLAGE – ORNAMENTS –

14.			
15.			
16.			

CHRISTMAS IN THE CITY – ORNAMENTS –

17.			
18.			
19.			

PENCIL TOTALS

20 New!

City Hall
Classic Ornament Series
Issued: 1998 • Current
#98771 • Orig. Price: $20
Market Value: $20

21

Dorothy's Dress Shop
Classic Ornament Series
Issued: 1997 • Retired: 1998
#98740 • Orig. Price: $15
Market Value: $17

22 New!

Dorothy's Dress Shop
Classic Ornament Series
Issued: 1998 • Current
#98770 • Orig. Price: $20
Market Value: $20

23 New!

Red Brick Fire Station
Classic Ornament Series
Issued: 1998 • Current
#98758 • Orig. Price: $20
Market Value: $20

24 New!

Elf Bunkhouse
Classic Ornament Series
Issued: 1998 • Current
#98763 • Orig. Price: $20
Market Value: $20

25

North Pole Santa's Workshop
Classic Ornament Series
Issued: 1997 • Retired: 1998
#98734 • Orig. Price: $16.50
Market Value: $19

26 New!

Reindeer Barn
Classic Ornament Series
Issued: 1998 • Current
#98762 • Orig. Price: $20
Market Value: $20

27

Santa's Lookout Tower
Classic Ornament Series
Issued: 1997 • Retired: 1998
#98742 • Orig. Price: $15
Market Value: $17

28 New!

Santa's Lookout Tower
Classic Ornament Series
Issued: 1998 • Current
#98773 • Orig. Price: $20
Market Value: $20

29 New!

Santa's Workshop
Classic Ornament Series
Issued: 1998 • Current
#98772 • Orig. Price: $22
Market Value: $22

CHRISTMAS IN THE CITY – ORNAMENTS –		
Year Purch.	Price Paid	Value Of My Collection
20.		
21.		
22.		
23.		
NORTH POLE – ORNAMENTS –		
24.		
25.		
26.		
27.		
28.		
29.		
PENCIL TOTALS		

CHRISTMAS/NORTH POLE – ORNAMENTS –

VALUE GUIDE – FUTURE RELEASES

Use this page to record future Heritage Village releases.

HERITAGE VILLAGE	Original Price	Status	Market Value	Year Purch.	Price Paid	Value of My Collection
PENCIL TOTALS						

TOTAL VALUE OF MY COLLECTION

Record the value of your collection here by adding the pencil totals from the bottom of each Value Guide page.

HERITAGE VILLAGE BUILDINGS		
Page Number	Price Paid	Market Value
Page 29		
Page 30		
Page 31		
Page 32		
Page 33		
Page 34		
Page 35		
Page 36		
Page 37		
Page 38		
Page 39		
Page 40		
Page 41		
Page 42		
Page 43		
Page 44		
Page 45		
Page 46		
Page 47		
Page 48		
Page 49		
Page 50		
Page 51		
Page 52		
Page 53		
Page 54		
TOTAL		

HERITAGE VILLAGE BUILDINGS		
Page Number	Price Paid	Market Value
Page 55		
Page 56		
Page 57		
Page 58		
Page 59		
Page 60		
Page 61		
Page 62		
Page 63		
Page 64		
Page 65		
Page 66		
Page 67		
Page 68		
Page 69		
Page 70		
Page 71		
Page 72		
Page 73		
Page 74		
Page 75		
Page 76		
Page 77		
Page 78		
Page 79		
Page 80		
Page 81		
TOTAL		

TOTAL VALUE OF MY COLLECTION

Record the value of your collection here by adding the pencil totals from the bottom of each Value Guide page.

HERITAGE VILLAGE ACCESSORIES

Page Number	Price Paid	Market Value
Page 82		
Page 83		
Page 84		
Page 85		
Page 86		
Page 87		
Page 88		
Page 89		
Page 90		
Page 91		
Page 92		
Page 93		
Page 94		
Page 95		
Page 96		
Page 97		
Page 98		
Page 99		
Page 100		
TOTAL		

HERITAGE VILLAGE ACCESSORIES

Page Number	Price Paid	Market Value
Page 101		
Page 102		
Page 103		
Page 104		
Page 105		
Page 106		
Page 107		
Page 108		
Page 109		
Page 110		
Page 111		
TOTAL		

HERITAGE VILLAGE HINGED BOXES & ORNAMENTS

Page Number	Price Paid	Market Value
Page 112		
Page 113		
Page 114		
Page 115		
TOTAL		

GRAND TOTALS

PRICE PAID	MARKET VALUE

$\mathcal{A}$ s the first "for sale" signs went up in gift and collectibles stores across the nation, collectors were drawn to several miniature buildings from Department 56 – the first releases in The Original Snow Village. The first lighted buildings (with relatively simple designs compared to today's buildings) were so unique that they immediately captured the imagination of collectors everywhere. This line catered to those with a vision: not just to create the perfect display, but to build their own dream village.

For many people, the magical allure of Snow Village comes from the feeling of nostalgia it invokes (even with collectors who didn't grow up in an era where "sock hops" and sledding were favorite American pastimes). Since the first introductions in 1976, Snow Village has grown to feature over 226 buildings and 179 accessories. And while Snow Village was originally set in the 1930s and 1940s, the town has now blossomed to encompass many modern facilities. So, not unlike many American towns, Snow Village has grown from a small grouping of homes and churches to include all the conveniences of modern society.

Part of Snow Village's initial charm was the rough, austere look the buildings had. Times change, however, and the village has transformed into a selection of elaborate pieces with both a grander scale and brighter, more vibrant colors. Other changes to the village include the growth of the line of accessories that you can use to personalize your village display. While the earliest pieces consisted of snow-laden trees and an occasional town resident, recent years have brought about a variety of larger, finely detailed accessories, some of which are even animated.

Snow Village differs from The Heritage Village Collection in three ways: first, all pieces (including accessories) finish their production process with a clear glaze. Therefore, instead of having a matte appearance, pieces have a shiny, almost satin, finish. The second is that all of the Snow Village pieces are ceramic, rather than porcelain. And finally, Snow Village is set apart from Heritage Village by the fact that there are no separate villages within Snow Village; all the pieces that bear the name are designed to be displayed together.

Also adding to the uniqueness of Snow Village is that since the early 1990s, Department 56 has entered into various licensing agreements that have allowed them to produce buildings and accessories bearing the names of familiar products. These products are part of everyday life and often help conjure up memories from our youth. Department 56 has received licenses from companies including Harley-Davidson®, Coca-Cola® and Hershey's™. And what town is complete without a car dealership? So, new for 1999, collectors can drive away with their very own Ford®.

An interesting group of buildings within Snow Village is featured in the *American Architecture Series.* This series features a variety of unique structures that are prime examples of different styles of American architecture. Each piece is named for the style that inspired the design. The series was first introduced in 1990 and still continues today, with this year's piece, "Stick Style House," marking the 10th release to date.

While in the past, various artists have designed for the Snow Village line, all pieces in the line are currently created by Department 56 artist Scott Enter. The magic he creates, coupled with the rustic styling of the early releases, all contribute to helping you create the town of your dreams; be it a quiet neighborhood complete with white picket fences or a bustling downtown area with a variety of shops – or both!

*C*heckerBee Publishing recently had the chance to ask Department 56 artist Scott Enter to share a little bit about what it's like to spend a workday designing the famous buildings that have entranced collectors for over 20 years. CheckerBee Publishing is honored that Mr. Enter took time out of his busy schedule to answer some questions about his life, his work and his love of design.

CHECKERBEE PUBLISHING: The designers of Department 56® Villages are understandably referred to as "architects." In the design process, do you find it helpful to formulate an interior floor plan to help you determine the exterior of the building?

SCOTT ENTER: You really do have to play the role of "architect" when designing Village pieces. For the houses, I often develop floor plans in my head to help me best envision how someone may really live there, and also to help guide some of the exterior features like the fireplace's chimney and the windows.

CHECKERBEE: What was the first building that you designed for Department 56 and what memories do you carry from that experience?

ENTER: "The Village Greenhouse," from The Original Snow Village® was the first lighted piece that I created. The Greenhouse started out as an accessory and once we saw the design, we realized what the magic of light would bring to it, so it became a lighted Village piece. After that, Department 56 felt I should be creating more pieces. All together, I have designed close to 100 lighted pieces and 30 accessories. I've been working with Department 56 for nine years and designing pieces for The Original Snow Village since 1990. I also have helped design other Village series pieces, along with general accessory items.

CHECKERBEE: A number of lighted pieces are replicas of real structures. Have you ever traveled to one of the buildings you've worked on and, if so, what was it like?

Interview With Scott Enter

ENTER: One real structure we have done that is dear to my heart – and stomach – is McDonald's®. Like most people, I have been eating McDonald's since I was a child. When creating this piece, I wanted to make sure that it had a lot of character and that collectors would be able to identify with it. We decided to create one of the original McDonald's for those very reasons. The really ironic thing about working on the McDonald's piece is that my first job when I was growing up was at McDonald's.

CHECKERBEE: Has a particular story or incident influenced a decision to create a particular building?

ENTER: So much of what we design is inspired by a story I've heard or read, but it is rarely visible in the end product. Occasionally, an anniversary or special event is the influence for a new piece, like the 95th anniversary of Harley-Davidson®.

> **"One creative person that I try to emulate is Norman Rockwell. . . . I want people to be able to identify with each piece I create and have them spark memories much like Rockwell's work is able to do."**

CHECKERBEE: Is there a particular building you would like to see produced in the future?

ENTER: There are a lot of buildings that I would like the opportunity to create in the future. One of the exciting parts of this job is the ability to have input in the selection process. If I were to tell you which pieces I would like to see, I run the risk of revealing our next piece. As Ms. Lit Town would say, "You'll just have to wait and see."

CHECKERBEE: Have you ever designed a piece that, for one reason or another, couldn't make it into the production schedule? If so, what happened to the design?

ENTER: I have been fortunate that all my designs have been produced. There have been times during the production process when a piece has been put on hold for one reason or another. But in the end, all of the pieces have been produced.

CHECKERBEE: How would you characterize yourself as an artist? Is there a creative person that you aspire to emulate?

ENTER: I would characterize myself as a very "hands-on" person. I like to be involved from start to finish in all my projects. One creative person that I try to emulate is Norman Rockwell. Rockwell had the ability to stir memories in others through his work. I want people to be able to identify with each piece I create and have them spark memories much like Rockwell's work is able to do.

CHECKERBEE: Who has played a significant role in how you developed as an artist?

ENTER: My father played a significant role in my career development. He always showed a lot of interest in what I was doing and encouraged me to enjoy my talents.

CHECKERBEE: What do you think you would be doing today if you had never pursued your interest in art and design?

ENTER: I might have been a contractor or a carpenter. It would have to be an occupation where I could work with my hands. I love working with my hands.

CHECKERBEE: How do you feel when you see a completed building? Is it usually what you imagined it would be or are you sometimes surprised by the final product?

ENTER: I am always very excited to see the completed pieces. It's like having a dream come to life – to see eight months of work come together makes it really rewarding. I'm never surprised by the final product because I work closely with the sculptors to ensure the image in my mind is captured in the final piece.

Interview With Scott Enter

CheckerBee: It is evident that attention to detail and historical accuracy are very important to Department 56. Can you take us through the research process that occurs when a new design is being considered?

Enter: Most of my designs are not based on specific buildings, but incorporate features of many buildings. Through readings, interviews and travel I gather research for my designs. I keep files of features I particularly like and sometimes use them years later on "just the right" building. Often, I incorporate many authentic features into one design.

CheckerBee: Who do you ask for advice when developing a design?

Enter: Ideas can come to me at many different times and places during the day, so I'm lucky to work closely with a really talented group of people. Often our ideas build on one another and that allows us to create fantastic pieces every year.

CheckerBee: What aspect of the design process do you enjoy the most?

Enter: There are definite rewards and challenges to each step of the design process, but there is gratification in every step. From concept to dealer showrooms, the entire process takes between eight months to a year. With the completion of each step, it's that much closer to the end result and the excitement grows as you see the piece come together.

CheckerBee: How do you decorate for the holidays?

Enter: My wife and I love the holiday season, therefore we try to make it as special as we can for the whole family. We decorate with lots of lights inside and out and use many Department 56 items. Of course, the highlight is our Department 56 Village collection scattered throughout the house.

*S*now Village is growing again with the addition of 10 buildings, 23 accessories and five ornaments.

SNOW VILLAGE BUILDINGS

. . . ANOTHER MAN'S TREASURE GARAGE (SET/22) . . .

Who knows what amazing things you can stumble upon at a garage sale? And this one is no exception, as it has everything from a pink flamingo for the yard to a butter churn, as well as coffee and donuts (fresh to eat, of course!).

CENTER FOR THE ARTS . . .

A little snow won't keep the folks of Snow Village from enjoying the arts. The "Center For The Arts" is three buildings in one, the Mackenzie Studio of Dance, Andrew's Art Supplies and the Alexander Gallery. The artistic inhabitants have decorated the building with wreaths, garland and a village scene in a front window, adding to the festive decor of downtown Snow Village.

THE FARMER'S CO-OP GRANARY . . .

This massive structure provides the farmers of Snow Village with plenty of feed to stock up for the cold winter months. Customers on the run can fill their orders at the door on the side of the building, while those who want to talk about town news are always welcome to go inside.

FIRE STATION #3 . . .

Constructed of bright red brick and accented in green, "Fire Station #3" resembles an old firehouse from days gone by. On one side of the building, a fire truck emerges from the garage ready for action, while the garage door on the other side is open, giving us a peek at the fire hose, axes, ladder and, of course, fire extinguisher, that are neatly arranged on the wall inside.

HARLEY-DAVIDSON® MANUFACTURING (SET/3) . . . Snow Village became "hog heaven" when the new Harley-Davidson plant arrived in town. Twin smokestacks reading "Harley" and "Davidson," along with the famous Harley-Davidson logo on the roof make the building a hard one to miss. An overhang on the side of the building protects two parked bikes, while another overhang guards a hog that's packed up and ready to be shipped.

HIDDEN PONDS HOUSE . . . Tucked in the heart of Snow Village, this cottage exudes a cozy warmth sure to make guests wish they didn't have to leave. The outside of the house is decorated with garland for the holidays. On one side, there's a bench tucked beneath latticework and greenery which provides a nice place to relax on lazy summer days.

LIONEL® ELECTRIC TRAIN SHOP . . . The year 2000 marks Lionel's 100-year anniversary of manufacturing model trains. Train lovers of all ages can help celebrate now that the new "Lionel® Electric Train Shop" is chugging its way into Snow Village. The shop offers the best model trains around, several of which are featured on a sign in the front window.

THE SECRET GARDEN GREENHOUSE . . . Snow Village residents can enjoy fresh greenery year-round now that "The Secret Garden Greenhouse" has opened. The glass walls allow customers to see the different kinds of flowers and plants to choose from. This piece was also released as "Bachman Greenhouse," an exclusive to the Bachman's Village Gathering in 1998 and is a companion piece to "The Secret Garden Florist."

STICK STYLE HOUSE . . . As the 10th piece in the *American Architecture Series*, the "Stick Style House" shows off the unique design elements characteristic of late 1800s architecture. Features such as wood panels, a gabled roof and a large porch add to the allure of this beautiful home, as does the warm green color.

UPTOWN MOTORS FORD® (SET/3) . . . When shopping for a new car, customers are sure to find the best deal when they visit "Uptown Motors Ford®." For those not quite ready to buy, you can peer through three huge glass windows at the new, bright red 1965 Ford Mustang as it rotates on the showroom floor. The brick building has two Ford flags on the rooftop, alongside the "Ford, Since 1930" sign. The set of three also includes a lighted Ford sign.

SNOW VILLAGE ACCESSORIES

Just beside the **"HARLEY-DAVIDSON® WATER TOWER,"** the **"UPTOWN MOTORS FORD® BILLBOARD"** lures customers onto the lot to see the **"1955 FORD® AUTOMOBILES,"** as well as the **"1964½ FORD® MUSTANG."** If someone should purchase a car, the mechanics always provide **"QUALITY SERVICE AT FORD®"** (set/2). Down the street, children are having **"FUN AT THE FIREHOUSE"** (set/2) with a fireman and the firehouse's dalmatians. If the kids are lucky, the fireman may even let them climb aboard the **"VILLAGE FIRE TRUCK."** Meanwhile, there's a **"FIREMAN TO THE RESCUE"** (set/3) to help a kitten who's stuck in a tree. A little boy and his father are outside playing with a new Lionel train they've already opened because they **"COULDN'T WAIT UNTIL CHRISTMAS."**

Getting ready for the cold weather, a **"FARMER'S FLATBED"** hauls grain and hay to stock

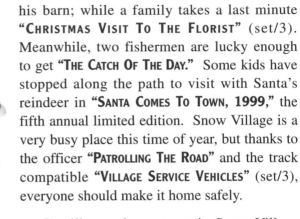

his barn; while a family takes a last minute **"Christmas Visit To The Florist"** (set/3). Meanwhile, two fishermen are lucky enough to get **"The Catch Of The Day."** Some kids have stopped along the path to visit with Santa's reindeer in **"Santa Comes To Town, 1999,"** the fifth annual limited edition. Snow Village is a very busy place this time of year, but thanks to the officer **"Patrolling The Road"** and the track compatible **"Village Service Vehicles"** (set/3), everyone should make it home safely.

It will soon be summer in Snow Village and that means time for garage sales where you just might find **" . . . Another Man's Treasure Accessories"** (set/3). It also means it's time to set up **"Uncle Sam's Fireworks Stand"** (set/2). And before you know it, the seasons will change again and there will be Halloween **"Costumes For Sale"** (set/2).

Wrapping up this year's releases are four new general village accessories; **"Ski Slope,"** **"Biplane Up In The Sky,"** **"Up, Up & Away Witch"** and the **"Village Express Electric Train Set"** (set/24).

Snow Village Ornaments

The ornaments released this year in the *Classic Ornament Series* are now lighted. Three of the new releases (**"Nantucket,"** **"Steepled Church"** and **"J. Young's Granary"**) were previously available without the lights. The other two releases, **"Lighthouse"** and **"Pinewood Log Cabin"** are new to the ornament series.

E ach year Department 56 announces the Snow Village retirements in *USA Today,* as well as on the official web site (*www.department56.com*). In 1998, collectors interested in their own copy of the announcement were allowed to pre-register to receive an e-mail on the morning of the retirements. The following Snow Village pieces (listed with issue year in parentheses) were retired on November 6, 1998.

SNOW VILLAGE BUILDINGS

❑ Beacon Hill Victorian (1995)
❑ Bowling Alley (1995)
❑ Coca-Cola® Brand Corner Drugstore (1995)
❑ Holly Brothers Garage (1995)
❑ New Hope Church (1997)
❑ Old Chelsea Mansion (1997)
❑ The Original Snow Village Start A Tradition Set (1997, set/8)
❑ Pisa Pizza (1995)
❑ Rock Creek Mill (1998)
❑ Rockabilly Records (1996)
❑ Skate & Ski Shop (1994)
❑ Snow Carnival Ice Palace (1995, set/2)
❑ Snowy Pines Inn (1998, set/9)
❑ Village Police Station (1995)

SNOW VILLAGE ACCESSORIES

❑ Christmas Trash Cans (1990, set/2)
❑ Classic Cars (1993, set/3)
❑ Coca-Cola® Brand Delivery Men (1994, set/2)
❑ Coca-Cola® Brand Delivery Truck (1994)
❑ Fire Hydrant And Mailbox (1988, set/2)

SNOW VILLAGE ACCESSORIES, cont.

❑ For Sale Sign (1989)
❑ Mailbox (1990)
❑ Men At Work (1996, set/5)
❑ Moving Day (1996, set/3)
❑ Parking Meter (1989, set/4)
❑ Pets On Parade (1994, set/2)
❑ Pizza Delivery (1995, set/2)
❑ Poinsettias For Sale (1995, set/3)
❑ Santa Comes To Town, 1998 (LE-1998)
❑ Service With A Smile (1995, set/2)
❑ Snow Carnival Ice Sculptures (1995, set/2)
❑ Snow Carnival King & Queen (1995)
❑ Stop Sign (1989, set/2)
❑ Stuck In The Snow (1994, set/3)
❑ Village Animated Ski Mountain (1996)
❑ Village Streetcar (1994, set/10)

CLASSIC ORNAMENT SERIES

❑ J. Young's Granary (1997)
❑ Nantucket (1997)
❑ Steepled Church (1997)

he following section lists the top 10 Snow Village pieces. The rank is established by each piece's value on the secondary market. Our market meter shows the percentage increase of each piece's value over the issue price.

CATHEDRAL CHURCH (#5067-4)
Issued 1980 • Retired 1981
Issue Price: $36 • Market Value: $2,650
Market Meter: +7,262%

This piece experienced many problems during construction, including the collapse of the dome during the firing.

ADOBE HOUSE (#5066-6)
Issued 1979 • Retired 1980
Issue Price: $18 • Market Value: $2,620
Market Meter: +14,456%

Due to its rough look, the "Adobe House" was not a favorite with collectors in 1979 when it was released.

MOBILE HOME (#5063-3)
Issued 1979 • Retired 1980
Issue Price: $18 • Market Value: $1,900
Market Meter: +10,456%

The "Mobile Home" is another piece not warmly welcomed during its availability, but it is now highly sought after.

MISSION CHURCH (#5062-5)
Issued 1979 • Retired 1980
Issue Price: $30 • Market Value: $1,275
Market Meter: +4,150%

The "Mission Church" is the second church in the Top 10 and was also retired after just one year of production.

SKATING RINK/DUCK POND SET (#5015-3)
Issued 1978 • Retired 1979
Issue Price: $16 • Market Value: $1,000
Market Meter: +6,150%

The way the trees were attached to the ponds made this piece quite fragile and caused it to break during shipment.

STONE CHURCH (#5059-1)
Issued 1979 • Retired 1980
Issue Price: $32 • Market Value: **$970**
Market Meter: +2,932%

Introduced in 1979, two years after the original "Stone Church," this piece differs from the first version in color and the amount of windows.

DINER (#5078-4)
Issued 1986 • Retired 1987
Issue Price: $22 • Market Value: **$660**
Market Meter: +2,900%

Referred to by many collectors as "Mickey's," this piece is a replica of a restaurant in the Minneapolis/St. Paul area.

BANK (#5024-5)
Issued 1982 • Retired 1983
Issue Price: $32 • Market Value: **$630**
Market Meter: +1,869%

This piece is hard to come by on the secondary market as it was sought after by bankers and collectors alike.

CONGREGATIONAL CHURCH (#5034-2)
Issued 1984 • Retired 1985
Issue Price: $28 • Market Value: **$625**
Market Meter: +2,133%

The "Congregational Church" was retired after just one year on store shelves due, in part, to the steeple breaking during shipment.

STONE CHURCH (#5009-6)
Issued 1977 • Retired 1979
Issue Price: $35 • Market Value: **$620**
Market Meter: +1,672%

This, the first version of "Stone Church," is the 1977 introduction featuring a lighter color that was available for only two years.

How To Use Your Collector's Value Guide™

1. **LOCATE** your piece in the Value Guide. This section lists all of The Original Snow Village buildings first, immediately followed by Snow Village accessories. All of the buildings and accessories are listed in alphabetical order and indexes are available in the back of the book to help you find your pieces.

56 Flavors Ice Cream Parlor
Issued: 1990 • Retired: 1992
#5151-9 • Original Price: $42
Market Value: $177

2. **FIND** the market value for your piece. If there is a variation of the piece with secondary market value, it is shown in the box as well (all versions are in chronological order). Any building or accessory for which a secondary market value has not been established is listed as "N/E." All pieces that are presently available in stores are listed with the current suggested retail price.

3. **RECORD** the date you purchased your piece as well as the price you paid and the current market value in the appropriate box located in the grid at the bottom of each Value Guide page.

4. **CALCULATE** the value for all the pieces you own on the page by adding together all of the boxes in each column. Be sure to use a pencil so you can change the totals as your collection grows!

SNOW VILLAGE – BUILDINGS –		
Year Purchased	Price Paid	Value Of My Collection
1. 9/8/91	42.00	177.00
2.		
3.		
4.		
5.		
PENCIL TOTALS		

5. **TRANSFER** the totals for each page in this section to the "Total Value Of My Collection" worksheet for Snow Village that can be found on page 189.

6. **ADD** all of the totals together on the worksheet so you can determine the overall value of your collection!

SNOW VILLAGE BUILDINGS

The Original Snow Village captures the story of a small town and brings it to life with its reproductions of small town America staples such as buildings, churches, homes and shops. The village boasts 227 buildings, making it the largest in Department 56. Currently, the most valuable Snow Village building is the "Cathedral Church" (1980), which is valued at more than $2,600.

1

56 Flavors Ice Cream Parlor
Issued: 1990 • Retired: 1992
#5151-9 • Original Price: $42
Market Value: $177

2

2101 Maple
Issued: 1986 • Retired: 1986
#5043-1 • Original Price: $32
Market Value: $350

3

Adobe House
Issued: 1979 • Retired: 1980
#5066-6 • Original Price: $18
Market Value: $2,620

4

Airport
Issued: 1992 • Retired: 1996
#5439-9 • Original Price: $60
Market Value: $87

5

Al's TV Shop
Issued: 1992 • Retired: 1995
#5423-2 • Original Price: $40
Market Value: $66

SNOW VILLAGE
– BUILDINGS –

	Year Purchased	Price Paid	Value Of My Collection
1.			
2.			
3.			
4.			
5.			
PENCIL TOTALS			

SNOW VILLAGE – BUILDINGS –

6

All Saints Church
Issued: 1986 • Retired: 1997
#5070-9 • Original Price: $38
Market Value: $58

7

New!

. . . Another Man's Treasure Garage (set/22)
Issued: 1998 • Current
#54945 • Original Price: $60
Market Value: $60

8

Apothecary
Issued: 1986 • Retired: 1990
#5076-8 • Original Price: $34
Market Value: $105

9

Bakery
Issued: 1981 • Retired: 1983
#5077-6 • Original Price: $30
Market Value: $280

10

Bakery
Issued: 1986 • Retired: 1991
#5077-6 • Original Price: $35
Market Value: $90

11

Bank
Issued: 1982 • Retired: 1983
#5024-5 • Original Price: $32
Market Value: $630

12

Barn
Issued: 1981 • Retired: 1984
#5074-1 • Original Price: $32
Market Value: $440

SNOW VILLAGE
– BUILDINGS –

	Year Purchased	Price Paid	Value Of My Collection
6.			
7.			
8.			
9.			
10.			
11.			
12.			
PENCIL TOTALS			

(13)

Bayport
Issued: 1984 • Retired: 1986
#5015-6 • Original Price: $30
Market Value: $230

(14)

Beacon Hill House
Issued: 1986 • Retired: 1988
#5065-2 • Original Price: $31
Market Value: $185

(15)

Beacon Hill Victorian
Issued: 1995 • Retired; 1998
#54857 • Original Price: $60
Market Value: $73

(16)

Birch Run Ski Chalet
Issued: 1996 • Current
#54882 • Original Price: $60
Market Value: $60

(17)

Boulder Springs House
Issued: 1996 • Retired: 1997
#54873 • Original Price: $60
Market Value: $75

(18)

Bowling Alley
Issued: 1995 • Retired: 1998
#54858 • Original Price: $42
Market Value: $52

(19)

The Brandon Bungalow
Issued: 1997 • Current
#54918 • Original Price: $55
Market Value: $55

SNOW VILLAGE – BUILDINGS –

	Year Purchased	Price Paid	Value Of My Collection
13.			
14.			
15.			
16.			
17.			
18.			
19.			
PENCIL TOTALS			

SNOW VILLAGE – BUILDINGS –

20

Brownstone
Issued: 1979 • Retired: 1981
#5056-7 • Original Price: $36
Market Value: $580

21

Cape Cod
Issued: 1978 • Retired: 1980
#5013-8 • Original Price: $20
Market Value: $385

22

Carmel Cottage
Issued: 1994 • Retired: 1997
#5466-6 • Original Price: $48
Market Value: $67

23

**The Carnival Carousel
(animated, musical)**
Issued: 1998 • Current
#54933 • Original Price: $150
Market Value: $150

24

Carriage House
Issued: 1982 • Retired: 1984
#5021-0 • Original Price: $28
Market Value: $325

25

Carriage House
Issued: 1986 • Retired: 1988
#5071-7 • Original Price: $29
Market Value: $128

26

Cathedral Church
Issued: 1980 • Retired: 1981
#5067-4 • Original Price: $36
Market Value: $2,650

SNOW VILLAGE
– BUILDINGS –

	Year Purchased	Price Paid	Value Of My Collection
20.			
21.			
22.			
23.			
24.			
25.			
26.			
PENCIL TOTALS			

27

Cathedral Church
Issued: 1987 • Retired: 1990
#5019-9 • Original Price: $50
Market Value: $113

28

Centennial House
Issued: 1982 • Retired: 1984
#5020-2 • Original Price: $32
Market Value: $335

29
New!

Center For The Arts
Issued: 1998 • Current
#54940 • Original Price: $64
Market Value: $64

30

Chateau
Issued: 1983 • Retired: 1984
#5084-9 • Original Price: $35
Market Value: $465

31

Christmas Barn Dance
Issued: 1997 • Current
#54910 • Original Price: $65
Market Value: $65

32

Christmas Cove Lighthouse
Issued: 1995 • Current
#5483-6 • Original Price: $60
Market Value: $60

33

Christmas Lake High School
Issued: 1996 • Current
#54881 • Original Price: $52
Market Value: $52

SNOW VILLAGE
– BUILDINGS –

	Year Purchased	Price Paid	Value Of My Collection
27.			
28.			
29.			
30.			
31.			
32.			
33.			
PENCIL TOTALS			

SNOW VILLAGE – BUILDINGS –

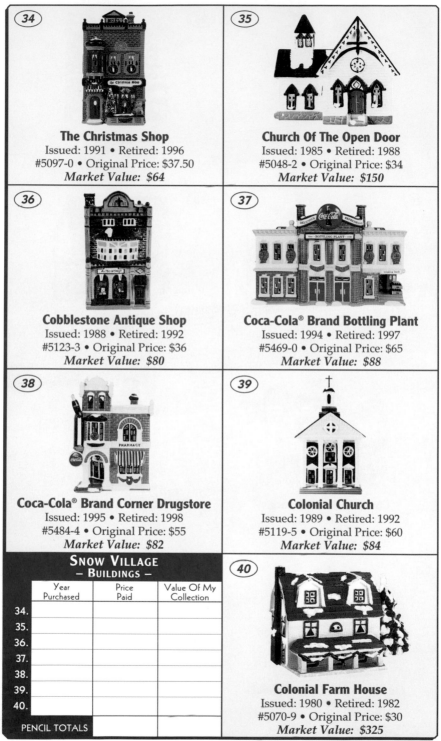

(34)

The Christmas Shop
Issued: 1991 • Retired: 1996
#5097-0 • Original Price: $37.50
Market Value: $64

(35)

Church Of The Open Door
Issued: 1985 • Retired: 1988
#5048-2 • Original Price: $34
Market Value: $150

(36)

Cobblestone Antique Shop
Issued: 1988 • Retired: 1992
#5123-3 • Original Price: $36
Market Value: $80

(37)

Coca-Cola® Brand Bottling Plant
Issued: 1994 • Retired: 1997
#5469-0 • Original Price: $65
Market Value: $88

(38)

Coca-Cola® Brand Corner Drugstore
Issued: 1995 • Retired: 1998
#5484-4 • Original Price: $55
Market Value: $82

(39)

Colonial Church
Issued: 1989 • Retired: 1992
#5119-5 • Original Price: $60
Market Value: $84

Snow Village
– Buildings –

	Year Purchased	Price Paid	Value Of My Collection
34.			
35.			
36.			
37.			
38.			
39.			
40.			
PENCIL TOTALS			

(40)

Colonial Farm House
Issued: 1980 • Retired: 1982
#5070-9 • Original Price: $30
Market Value: $325

(41)

Congregational Church
Issued: 1984 • Retired: 1985
#5034-2 • Original Price: $28
Market Value: $625

(42)

Corner Cafe
Issued: 1988 • Retired: 1991
#5124-1 • Original Price: $37
Market Value: $100

(43)

Corner Store
Issued: 1981 • Retired: 1983
#5076-8 • Original Price: $30
Market Value: $255

(44)

Country Church
Issued: 1976 • Retired: 1979
#5004-7 • Original Price: $18
Market Value: $370

(45)

Countryside Church
Issued: 1979 • Retired: 1984
#5058-3 • Original Price: $27.50
Market Value: $278

(46)

Courthouse
Issued: 1989 • Retired: 1993
#5144-6 • Original Price: $65
Market Value: $190

(47)

Craftsman Cottage
American Architecture Series
Issued: 1992 • Retired: 1995
#5437-2 • Original Price: $55
Market Value: $80

SNOW VILLAGE — BUILDINGS

SNOW VILLAGE
– BUILDINGS –

	Year Purchased	Price Paid	Value Of My Collection
41.			
42.			
43.			
44.			
45.			
46.			
47.			
PENCIL TOTALS			

48

Cumberland House
Issued: 1987 • Retired: 1995
#5024-5 • Original Price: $42
Market Value: $77

49

Dairy Barn
Issued: 1993 • Retired: 1997
#5446-1 • Original Price: $55
Market Value: $75

50

Delta House
Issued: 1984 • Retired: 1986
#5012-1 • Original Price: $32
Market Value: $320

51

Depot & Train With Two Train Cars (set/2)
Issued: 1985 • Retired: 1988
#5051-2 • Original Price: $65
Market Value: $155

52

Dinah's Drive-In
Issued: 1993 • Retired: 1996
#5447-0 • Original Price: $45
Market Value: $105

53

Diner
Issued: 1986 • Retired: 1987
#5078-4 • Original Price: $22
Market Value: $660

54

Doctor's House
Issued: 1989 • Retired: 1992
#5143-8 • Original Price: $56
Market Value: $103

SNOW VILLAGE
– BUILDINGS –

	Year Purchased	Price Paid	Value Of My Collection
48.			
49.			
50.			
51.			
52.			
53.			
54.			
PENCIL TOTALS			

55

Double Bungalow
Issued: 1991 • Retired: 1994
#5407-0 • Original Price: $45
Market Value: $67

56

Duplex
Issued: 1985 • Retired: 1987
#5050-4 • Original Price: $35
Market Value: $158

57

Dutch Colonial
American Architecture Series
Issued: 1995 • Retired: 1996
#54856 • Original Price: $45
Market Value: $65

58

English Church
Issued: 1981 • Retired: 1982
#5078-4 • Original Price: $30
Market Value: $380

59

English Cottage
Issued: 1981 • Retired: 1982
#5073-3 • Original Price: $25
Market Value: $300

60

English Tudor
Issued: 1983 • Retired: 1985
#5033-4 • Original Price: $30
Market Value: $287

61

Farm House
Issued: 1987 • Retired: 1992
#5089-0 • Original Price: $40
Market Value: $77

SNOW VILLAGE
– BUILDINGS –

	Year Purchased	Price Paid	Value Of My Collection
55.			
56.			
57.			
58.			
59.			
60.			
61.			
PENCIL TOTALS			

SNOW VILLAGE – BUILDINGS –

62

Farm House
Issued: 1997 • Current
#54912 • Original Price: $50
Market Value: $50

63
New!

The Farmer's Co-op Granary
Issued: 1998 • Current
#54946 • Original Price: $64
Market Value: $64

64

Federal House
American Architecture Series
Issued: 1994 • Retired: 1997
#5465-8 • Original Price: $50
Market Value: $72

65

Finklea's Finery: Costume Shop
Issued: 1991 • Retired: 1993
#5405-4 • Original Price: $45
Market Value: $69

66

Fire Station
Issued: 1983 • Retired: 1984
#5032-6 • Original Price: $32
Market Value: $615

67

Fire Station No. 2
Issued: 1987 • Retired: 1989
#5091-1 • Original Price: $40
Market Value: $210

SNOW VILLAGE
– BUILDINGS –

	Year Purchased	Price Paid	Value Of My Collection
62.			
63.			
64.			
65.			
66.			
67.			
68.			
PENCIL TOTALS			

68
New!

Fire Station #3
Issued: 1998 • Current
#54942 • Original Price: $70
Market Value: $70

69 Bass   Trout

Fisherman's Nook Cabins (set/2)
Issued: 1994 • Current
#5461-5 • Original Price: $50
Market Value: $50

70

Fisherman's Nook Resort
Issued: 1994 • Current
#5460-7 • Original Price: $75
Market Value: $75

71

Flower Shop
Issued: 1982 • Retired: 1983
#5082-2 • Original Price: $25
Market Value: $475

72

Gabled Cottage
Issued: 1976 • Retired: 1979
#5002-1 • Original Price: $20
Market Value: $375

73

Gabled House
Issued: 1982 • Retired: 1983
#5081-4 • Original Price: $30
Market Value: $400

74

Galena House
Issued: 1984 • Retired: 1985
#5009-1 • Original Price: $32
Market Value: $365

SNOW VILLAGE
— BUILDINGS —

	Year Purchased	Price Paid	Value Of My Collection
69.			
70.			
71.			
72.			
73.			
74.			
PENCIL TOTALS			

SNOW VILLAGE — BUILDINGS —

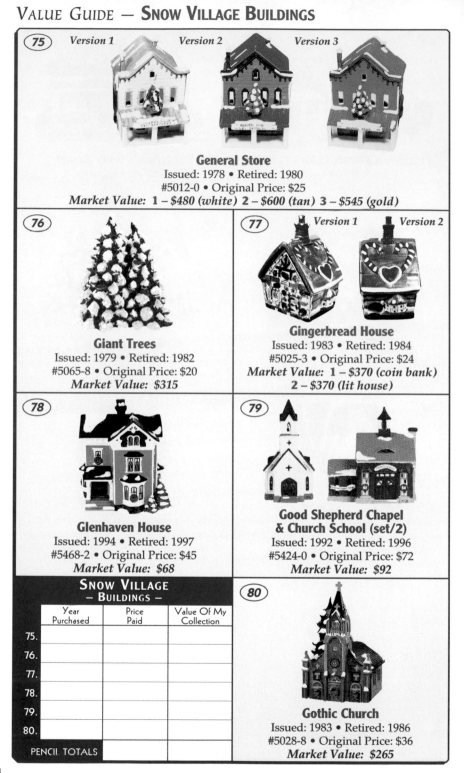

(75) Version 1   Version 2   Version 3

General Store
Issued: 1978 • Retired: 1980
#5012-0 • Original Price: $25
Market Value: **1** – *$480 (white)* **2** – *$600 (tan)* **3** – *$545 (gold)*

(76)

Giant Trees
Issued: 1979 • Retired: 1982
#5065-8 • Original Price: $20
Market Value: $315

(77) Version 1   Version 2

Gingerbread House
Issued: 1983 • Retired: 1984
#5025-3 • Original Price: $24
Market Value: **1** – *$370 (coin bank)*
2 – *$370 (lit house)*

(78)

Glenhaven House
Issued: 1994 • Retired: 1997
#5468-2 • Original Price: $45
Market Value: $68

(79)

Good Shepherd Chapel
& Church School (set/2)
Issued: 1992 • Retired: 1996
#5424-0 • Original Price: $72
Market Value: $92

SNOW VILLAGE
– BUILDINGS –

	Year Purchased	Price Paid	Value Of My Collection
75.			
76.			
77.			
78.			
79.			
80.			
PENCIL TOTALS			

(80)

Gothic Church
Issued: 1983 • Retired: 1986
#5028-8 • Original Price: $36
Market Value: $265

81

Gothic Farmhouse
American Architecture Series
Issued: 1991 • Retired: 1997
#5404-6 • Original Price: $48
Market Value: $66

82

Governor's Mansion
Issued: 1983 • Retired: 1985
#5003-2 • Original Price: $32
Market Value: $320

83

Gracie's Dry Goods
& General Store (set/2)
Issued: 1997 • Current
#54915 • Original Price: $70
Market Value: $70

84

Grandma's Cottage
Issued: 1992 • Retired: 1996
#5420-8 • Original Price: $42
Market Value: $68

85

Grocery
Issued: 1983 • Retired: 1985
#5001-6 • Original Price: $35
Market Value: $365

86
New!

Harley-Davidson® Manufacturing
(set/3)
Issued: 1998 • Current
#54948 • Original Price: $80
Market Value: $80

87

Harley-Davidson® Motorcycle Shop
Issued: 1996 • Current
#54886 • Original Price: $65
Market Value: $65

SNOW VILLAGE
– BUILDINGS –

	Year Purchased	Price Paid	Value Of My Collection
81.			
82.			
83.			
84.			
85.			
86.			
87.			
PENCIL TOTALS			

SNOW VILLAGE – BUILDINGS –

145

Value Guide — Snow Village Buildings

(88)

Hartford House
Issued: 1992 • Retired: 1995
#5426-7 • Original Price: $55
Market Value: $86

(89)

Haunted Mansion (animated)
Issued: 1998 • Current
#54935 • Original Price: $110
Market Value: $110

(90)

Haversham House
Issued: 1984 • Retired: 1987
#5008-3 • Original Price: $37
Market Value: $285

(91)

Hershey's™ Chocolate Shop
Issued: 1997 • Current
#54913 • Original Price: $55
Market Value: $55

(92) *New!*

Hidden Ponds House
Issued: 1998 • Current
#54944 • Original Price: $50
Market Value: $50

(93)

Highland Park House
Issued: 1986 • Retired: 1988
#5063-6 • Original Price: $35
Market Value: $155

SNOW VILLAGE
– BUILDINGS –

	Year Purchased	Price Paid	Value Of My Collection
88.			
89.			
90.			
91.			
92.			
93.			
94.			
PENCIL TOTALS			

(94)

Holly Brothers Garage
Issued: 1995 • Retired: 1998
#54854 • Original Price: $48
Market Value: $56

95

**Home Sweet Home/
House & Windmill (set/2)**
Issued: 1988 • Retired: 1991
#5126-8 • Original Price: $60
Market Value: $125

96

Homestead
Issued: 1978 • Retired: 1984
#5011-2 • Original Price: $30
Market Value: $255

97

The Honeymooner Motel
Issued: 1991 • Retired: 1993
#5401-1 • Original Price: $42
Market Value: $90

98

Hunting Lodge
Issued: 1993 • Retired: 1996
#5445-3 • Original Price: $50
Market Value: $145

99

The Inn
Issued: 1976 • Retired: 1979
#5003-9 • Original Price: $20
Market Value: $480

100

Italianate Villa
American Architecture Series
Issued: 1997 • Current
#54911 • Original Price: $55
Market Value: $55

101

J. Young's Granary
Issued: 1989 • Retired: 1992
#5149-7 • Original Price: $45
Market Value: $92

SNOW VILLAGE
— BUILDINGS —

	Year Purchased	Price Paid	Value Of My Collection
95.			
96.			
97.			
98.			
99.			
100.			
101.			
PENCIL TOTALS			

SNOW VILLAGE
— BUILDINGS —

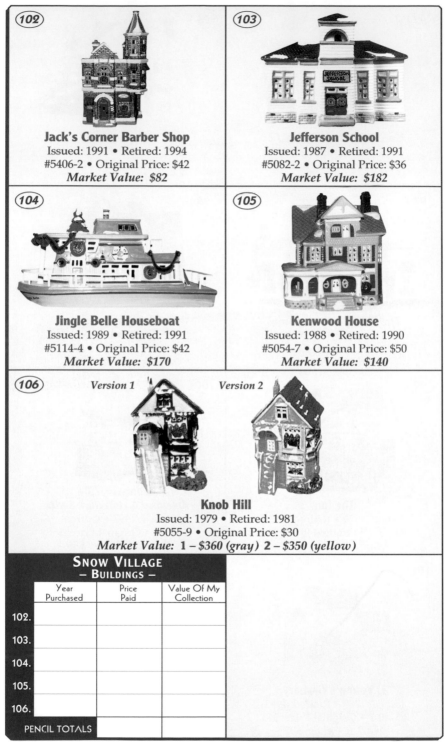

102

Jack's Corner Barber Shop
Issued: 1991 • Retired: 1994
#5406-2 • Original Price: $42
Market Value: $82

103

Jefferson School
Issued: 1987 • Retired: 1991
#5082-2 • Original Price: $36
Market Value: $182

104

Jingle Belle Houseboat
Issued: 1989 • Retired: 1991
#5114-4 • Original Price: $42
Market Value: $170

105

Kenwood House
Issued: 1988 • Retired: 1990
#5054-7 • Original Price: $50
Market Value: $140

106   Version 1   Version 2

Knob Hill
Issued: 1979 • Retired: 1981
#5055-9 • Original Price: $30
Market Value: 1 – $360 (gray) 2 – $350 (yellow)

SNOW VILLAGE
– BUILDINGS –

	Year Purchased	Price Paid	Value Of My Collection
102.			
103.			
104.			
105.			
106.			
PENCIL TOTALS			

(107)

Large Single Tree
Issued: 1981 • Retired: 1989
#5080-6 • Original Price: $17
Market Value: $58

(108)

Lighthouse
Issued: 1987 • Retired: 1988
#5030-0 • Original Price: $36
Market Value: $580

(109)

Lincoln Park Duplex
Issued: 1986 • Retired: 1988
#5060-1 • Original Price: $33
Market Value: $140

(110)

Linden Hills Country Club (set/2)
Issued: 1997 • Current
#54917 • Original Price: $60
Market Value: $60

(111)
New!

Version 1

Version 2

Lionel® Electric Train Shop
Issued: 1998 • Current
#54947 • Original Price: $55
Market Value: 1 – N/E (Allied Model Trains) 2 – $55 (general release)

(112)

Log Cabin
Issued: 1979 • Retired: 1981
#5057-5 • Original Price: $22
Market Value: $500

SNOW VILLAGE
– BUILDINGS –

	Year Purchased	Price Paid	Value Of My Collection
107.			
108.			
109.			
110.			
111.			
112.			
PENCIL TOTALS			

SNOW VILLAGE – BUILDINGS –

(113)

Main Street House
Issued: 1984 • Retired: 1986
#5005-9 • Original Price: $27
Market Value: $245

(114)

Mainstreet Gift Shop (GCC Piece)
Issued: 1997 • Retired: 1997
#54887 • Original Price: $50
Market Value: $93

(115)

Mainstreet Hardware Store
Issued: 1990 • Retired: 1993
#5153-5 • Original Price: $42
Market Value: $87

(116)

Mansion
Issued: 1977 • Retired: 1979
#5008-8 • Original Price: $30
Market Value: $520

(117)

Maple Ridge Inn
Issued: 1988 • Retired: 1990
#5121-7 • Original Price: $55
Market Value: $85

(118)

Marvel's Beauty Salon
Issued: 1994 • Retired: 1997
#5470-4 • Original Price: $37.50
Market Value: $60

SNOW VILLAGE
– BUILDINGS –

	Year Purchased	Price Paid	Value Of My Collection
113.			
114.			
115.			
116.			
117.			
118.			
119.			
PENCIL TOTALS			

(119)

McDonald's®
Issued: 1997 • Current
#54914 • Original Price: $65
Market Value: $65

120

Mission Church
Issued: 1979 • Retired: 1980
#5062-5 • Original Price: $30
Market Value: $1,275

121

Mobile Home
Issued: 1979 • Retired: 1980
#5063-3 • Original Price: $18
Market Value: $1,900

122

Morningside House
Issued: 1990 • Retired: 1992
#5152-7 • Original Price: $45
Market Value: $72

123

Mount Olivet Church
Issued: 1993 • Retired: 1996
#5442-9 • Original Price: $65
Market Value: $77

124

Mountain Lodge
Issued: 1976 • Retired: 1979
#5001-3 • Original Price: $20
Market Value: $385

125

Nantucket
Issued: 1978 • Retired: 1986
#5014-6 • Original Price: $25
Market Value: $265

126

Nantucket Renovation (LE-1993)
Issued: 1993 • Retired: 1993
#5441-0 • Original Price: $55
Market Value: $80

SNOW VILLAGE
– BUILDINGS –

	Year Purchased	Price Paid	Value Of My Collection
120.			
121.			
122.			
123.			
124.			
125.			
126.			
PENCIL TOTALS			

SNOW VILLAGE – BUILDINGS –

(127) New Hope Church
Issued: 1997 • Retired: 1998
#54904 • Original Price: $60
Market Value: $69

(128) New School House
Issued: 1984 • Retired: 1986
#5037-7 • Original Price: $35
Market Value: $260

(129) New Stone Church
Issued: 1982 • Retired: 1984
#5083-0 • Original Price: $32
Market Value: $372

(130) Nick's Tree Farm (set/10)
Nick The Tree Farmer   *Nick's Tree Farm*
Issued: 1996 • Current
#54871 • Original Price: $40
Market Value: $40

(131) North Creek Cottage
Issued: 1989 • Retired: 1992
#5120-9 • Original Price: $45
Market Value: $74

(132) Oak Grove Tudor
Issued: 1991 • Retired: 1994
#5400-3 • Original Price: $42
Market Value: $68

SNOW VILLAGE
– BUILDINGS –

	Year Purchased	Price Paid	Value Of My Collection
127.			
128.			
129.			
130.			
131.			
132.			
133.			
PENCIL TOTALS			

(133) Old Chelsea Mansion (with book)
Issued: 1997 • Retired: 1998
#54903 • Original Price: $85
Market Value: $105

(134)

Kringle's Toy Shop

Nikki's Cocoa Shop

Saturday Morning Downtown

The Original Snow Village Start A Tradition Set (set/8)
Issued: 1997 • Retired: 1998
#54902 • Original Price: $75
Market Value: $100

(135)

Pacific Heights House
Issued: 1986 • Retired: 1988
#5066-0 • Original Price: $33
Market Value: $105

(136)

Palos Verdes
Issued: 1988 • Retired: 1990
#5141-1 • Original Price: $37.50
Market Value: $85

(137)

Paramount Theater
Issued: 1989 • Retired: 1993
#5142-0 • Original Price: $42
Market Value: $182

(138)

Parish Church
Issued: 1984 • Retired: 1986
#5039-3 • Original Price: $32
Market Value: $327

(139)

Parsonage
Issued: 1983 • Retired: 1985
#5029-6 • Original Price: $35
Market Value: $370

(140)

Peppermint Porch Day Care
Issued: 1995 • Retired: 1997
#5485-2 • Original Price: $45
Market Value: $62

SNOW VILLAGE
– BUILDINGS –

	Year Purchased	Price Paid	Value Of My Collection
134.			
135.			
136.			
137.			
138.			
139.			
140.			
PENCIL TOTALS			

(Side tab) SNOW VILLAGE – BUILDINGS –

(141)

Pinewood Log Cabin
Issued: 1989 • Retired: 1995
#5150-0 • Original Price: $37.50
Market Value: $72

(142)

Pioneer Church
Issued: 1982 • Retired: 1984
#5022-9 • Original Price: $30
Market Value: $352

(143)

Pisa Pizza
Issued: 1995 • Retired: 1998
#54851 • Original Price: $35
Market Value: $45

(144)

Plantation House
Issued: 1985 • Retired: 1987
#5047-4 • Original Price: $37
Market Value: $114

(145)

Prairie House
American Architecture Series
Issued: 1990 • Retired: 1993
#5156-0 • Original Price: $42
Market Value: $75

(146)

Print Shop & Village News
Issued: 1992 • Retired: 1994
#5425-9 • Original Price: $37.50
Market Value: $80

SNOW VILLAGE
– BUILDINGS –

	Year Purchased	Price Paid	Value Of My Collection
141.			
142.			
143.			
144.			
145.			
146.			
147.			
PENCIL TOTALS			

(147)

Queen Anne Victorian
American Architecture Series
Issued: 1990 • Retired: 1996
#5157-8 • Original Price: $48
Market Value: $73

(148)

Ramsey Hill House
Issued: 1986 • Retired: 1989
#5067-9 • Original Price: $36
Market Value: $107

(149)

Red Barn
Issued: 1987 • Retired: 1992
#5081-4 • Original Price: $38
Market Value: $104

(150)

Redeemer Church
Issued: 1988 • Retired: 1992
#5127-6 • Original Price: $42
Market Value: $75

(151)

Reindeer Bus Depot
Issued: 1996 • Retired: 1997
#54874 • Original Price: $42
Market Value: $62

(152)

Ridgewood
Issued: 1985 • Retired: 1987
#5052-0 • Original Price: $35
Market Value: $174

(153)

River Road House
Issued: 1984 • Retired: 1987
#5010-5 • Original Price: $36
Market Value: $215

(154)

Rock Creek Mill
Issued: 1998 • Retired: 1998
#54932 • Original Price: $64
Market Value: $115

SNOW VILLAGE
— BUILDINGS —

	Year Purchased	Price Paid	Value Of My Collection
148.			
149.			
150.			
151.			
152.			
153.			
154.			
PENCIL TOTALS			

SNOW VILLAGE — BUILDINGS —

155

155

Rockabilly Records
Issued: 1996 • Retired: 1998
#54880 • Original Price: $45
Market Value: $54

156

Rollerama Roller Rink
Issued: 1997 • Current
#54916 • Original Price: $56
Market Value: $56

157

Rosita's Cantina
Issued: 1996 • Current
#54883 • Original Price: $50
Market Value: $50

158

Ryman Auditorium®
Issued: 1995 • Retired: 1997
#54855 • Original Price: $75
Market Value: $93

159

St. Anthony Hotel & Post Office
Issued: 1987 • Retired: 1989
#5006-7 • Original Price: $40
Market Value: $116

160

Saint James Church
Issued: 1986 • Retired: 1988
#5068-7 • Original Price: $37
Market Value: $172

161

St. Luke's Church
Issued: 1992 • Retired: 1994
#5421-6 • Original Price: $45
Market Value: $75

SNOW VILLAGE
– BUILDINGS –

	Year Purchased	Price Paid	Value Of My Collection
155.			
156.			
157.			
158.			
159.			
160.			
161.			
PENCIL TOTALS			

(162)

School House
Issued: 1979 • Retired: 1982
#5060-9 • Original Price: $30
Market Value: $382

(163)

The Secret Garden Florist
Issued: 1996 • Current
#54885 • Original Price: $50
Market Value: $50

(164)
New!

The Secret Garden Greenhouse
Issued: 1998 • Current
#54949 • Original Price: $60
Market Value: $60

(165)

Service Station
Issued: 1988 • Retired: 1991
#5128-4 • Original Price: $37.50
Market Value: $268

(166)

Shingle Victorian
American Architecture Series
Issued: 1996 • Current
#54884 • Original Price: $55
Market Value: $55

(167)

Single Car Garage
Issued: 1988 • Retired: 1990
#5125-0 • Original Price: $22
Market Value: $60

Snow Village
– Buildings –

	Year Purchased	Price Paid	Value Of My Collection
162.			
163.			
164.			
165.			
166.			
167.			
PENCIL TOTALS			

Snow Village – Buildings –

157

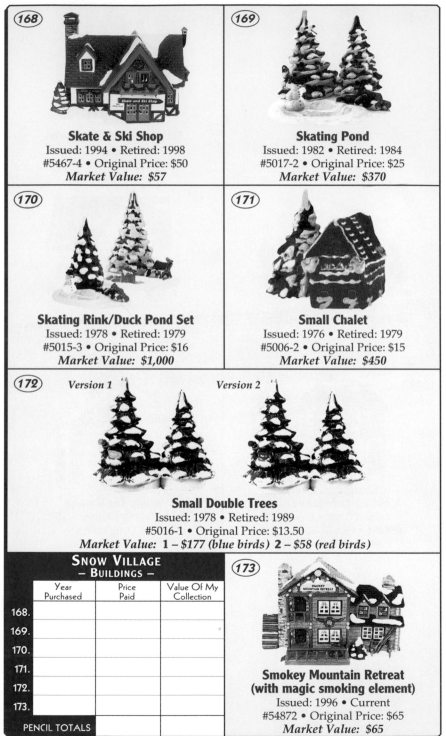

(168)

Skate & Ski Shop
Issued: 1994 • Retired: 1998
#5467-4 • Original Price: $50
Market Value: $57

(169)

Skating Pond
Issued: 1982 • Retired: 1984
#5017-2 • Original Price: $25
Market Value: $370

(170)

Skating Rink/Duck Pond Set
Issued: 1978 • Retired: 1979
#5015-3 • Original Price: $16
Market Value: $1,000

(171)

Small Chalet
Issued: 1976 • Retired: 1979
#5006-2 • Original Price: $15
Market Value: $450

(172)   Version 1   Version 2

Small Double Trees
Issued: 1978 • Retired: 1989
#5016-1 • Original Price: $13.50
Market Value: 1 – $177 (blue birds) 2 – $58 (red birds)

SNOW VILLAGE
– BUILDINGS –

	Year Purchased	Price Paid	Value Of My Collection
168.			
169.			
170.			
171.			
172.			
173.			
PENCIL TOTALS			

(173)

Smokey Mountain Retreat
(with magic smoking element)
Issued: 1996 • Current
#54872 • Original Price: $65
Market Value: $65

(174)

Snow Carnival Ice Palace (set/2)
Issued: 1995 • Retired: 1998
#54850 • Original Price: $95
Market Value: $110

(175)

Snow Village Factory
Issued: 1987 • Retired: 1989
#5013-0 • Original Price: $45
Market Value: $140

(176)

Snow Village Resort Lodge
Issued: 1987 • Retired: 1989
#5092-0 • Original Price: $55
Market Value: $144

(177)

Shady Oak Church

Sunday School Serenade

Snow Village Starter Set (set/6)
Issued: 1994 • Retired: 1996
#5462-3 • Original Price: $50
Market Value: $82

(178)

Snowy Hills Hospital
Issued: 1993 • Retired: 1996
#5448-8 • Original Price: $48
Market Value: $88

(179)

Snowy Pines Inn

Decorate The Tree

Snowy Pines Inn (set/9, Event Piece)
Issued: 1998 • Retired: 1998
#54934 • Original Price: $65
Market Value: $73

(180)

Sonoma House
Issued: 1986 • Retired: 1988
#5062-8 • Original Price: $33
Market Value: $150

SNOW VILLAGE
– BUILDINGS –

	Year Purchased	Price Paid	Value Of My Collection
174.			
175.			
176.			
177.			
178.			
179.			
180.			
PENCIL TOTALS			

Sidebar: SNOW VILLAGE – BUILDINGS –

181

Southern Colonial
American Architecture Series
Issued: 1991 • Retired: 1994
#5403-8 • Original Price: $50
Market Value: $82

182

Spanish Mission Church
Issued: 1990 • Retired: 1992
#5155-1 • Original Price: $42
Market Value: $84

183

Springfield House
Issued: 1987 • Retired: 1990
#5027-0 • Original Price: $40
Market Value: $86

184

Spruce Place
Issued: 1985 • Retired: 1987
#5049-0 • Original Price: $33
Market Value: $260

185

Starbucks® Coffee
Issued: 1995 • Current
#54859 • Original Price: $48
Market Value: $48

186

Steepled Church
Issued: 1976 • Retired: 1979
#5005-4 • Original Price: $25
Market Value: $560

Snow Village
– Buildings –

	Year Purchased	Price Paid	Value Of My Collection
181.			
182.			
183.			
184.			
185.			
186.			
187.			
PENCIL TOTALS			

187

New!

Stick Style House
American Architecture Series
Issued: 1998 • Current
#54943 • Original Price: $60
Market Value: $60

188

Stone Church
Issued: 1977 • Retired: 1979
#5009-6 • Original Price: $35
Market Value: $620

189

Stone Church
Issued: 1979 • Retired: 1980
#5059-1 • Original Price: $32
Market Value: $970

190

Stone Mill House
Issued: 1980 • Retired: 1982
#5068-2 • Original Price: $30
Market Value: $545

191

Stonehurst House
Issued: 1988 • Retired: 1994
#5140-3 • Original Price: $37.50
Market Value: $69

192

Stratford House
Issued: 1984 • Retired: 1986
#5007-5 • Original Price: $28
Market Value: $178

193

Street Car
Issued: 1982 • Retired: 1984
#5019-9 • Original Price: $16
Market Value: $375

SNOW VILLAGE – BUILDINGS –

SNOW VILLAGE
– BUILDINGS –

	Year Purchased	Price Paid	Value Of My Collection
188.			
189.			
190.			
191.			
192.			
193.			
PENCIL TOTALS			

(194)

Stucco Bungalow
Issued: 1985 • Retired: 1986
#5045-8 • Original Price: $30
Market Value: $375

(195)

Summit House
Issued: 1984 • Retired: 1985
#5036-9 • Original Price: $28
Market Value: $355

(196)

Swiss Chalet
Issued: 1982 • Retired: 1984
#5023-7 • Original Price: $28
Market Value: $438

(197)

Town Church
Issued: 1980 • Retired: 1982
#5071-7 • Original Price: $33
Market Value: $362

(198)

Town Hall
Issued: 1983 • Retired: 1984
#5000-8 • Original Price: $32
Market Value: $345

(199)

Toy Shop
Issued: 1986 • Retired: 1990
#5073-3 • Original Price: $36
Market Value: $97

SNOW VILLAGE
– BUILDINGS –

	Year Purchased	Price Paid	Value Of My Collection
194.			
195.			
196.			
197.			
198.			
199.			
PENCIL TOTALS			

200 Version 1 Version 2

Train Station With 3 Train Cars (set/4)
Issued: 1980 • Retired: 1985
#5085-6 • Original Price: $100
Market Value: **1** – *$400 (6 window panes/1 round window in door)*
2 – *$360 (8 window panes/2 square windows in door)*

201

Trinity Church
Issued: 1984 • Retired: 1986
#5035-0 • Original Price: $32
Market Value: $300

202

Tudor House
Issued: 1979 • Retired: 1981
#5061-7 • Original Price: $25
Market Value: $312

203

Turn Of The Century
Issued: 1983 • Retired: 1986
#5004-0 • Original Price: $36
Market Value: $265

204

Twin Peaks
Issued: 1986 • Retired: 1986
#5042-3 • Original Price: $32
Market Value: $460

205
New!

Uptown Motors Ford® (set/3)
Issued: 1998 • Current
#54941 • Original Price: $95
Market Value: $95

SNOW VILLAGE
— BUILDINGS —

	Year Purchased	Price Paid	Value Of My Collection
200.			
201.			
202.			
203.			
204.			
205.			
PENCIL TOTALS			

SNOW VILLAGE – BUILDINGS –

163

Value Guide — Snow Village Buildings

206

Victorian
Issued: 1979 • Retired: 1982
#5054-2 • Original Price: $30
Market Value: $350

207

Victorian Cottage
Issued: 1983 • Retired: 1984
#5002-4 • Original Price: $35
Market Value: $350

208

Victorian House
Issued: 1977 • Retired: 1979
#5007-0 • Original Price: $30
Market Value: $455

209

Village Church
Issued: 1983 • Retired: 1984
#5026-1 • Original Price: $30
Market Value: $425

210

Village Greenhouse
Issued: 1991 • Retired: 1995
#5402-0 • Original Price: $35
Market Value: $69

211

Village Market
Issued: 1988 • Retired: 1991
#5044-0 • Original Price: $39
Market Value: $87

Snow Village
– Buildings –

	Year Purchased	Price Paid	Value Of My Collection
206.			
207.			
208.			
209.			
210.			
211.			
212.			
PENCIL TOTALS			

212

Village Police Station
Issued: 1995 • Retired: 1998
#54853 • Original Price: $48
Market Value: $55

164

(213)

Village Post Office
Issued: 1992 • Retired: 1995
#5422-4 • Original Price: $35
Market Value: $75

(214)

Village Public Library
Issued: 1993 • Retired: 1997
#5443-7 • Original Price: $55
Market Value: $64

(215)

Village Realty
Issued: 1990 • Retired: 1993
#5154-3 • Original Price: $42
Market Value: $77

(216)

Village Station
Issued: 1992 • Retired: 1997
#5438-0 • Original Price: $65
Market Value: $75

(217)

Village Station And Train (set/2)
Issued: 1988 • Retired: 1992
#5122-5 • Original Price: $65
Market Value: $110

(218)

Village Vet And Pet Shop
Issued: 1992 • Retired: 1995
#5427-5 • Original Price: $32
Market Value: $76

(219)

Village Warming House
Issued: 1989 • Retired: 1992
#5145-4 • Original Price: $42
Market Value: $80

SNOW VILLAGE
– BUILDINGS –

	Year Purchased	Price Paid	Value Of My Collection
213.			
214.			
215.			
216.			
217.			
218.			
219.			
PENCIL TOTALS			

(side tab:) SNOW VILLAGE – BUILDINGS –

220

Waverly Place
Issued: 1986 • Retired: 1986
#5041-5 • Original Price: $35
Market Value: $305

221

Wedding Chapel
Issued: 1994 • Current
#5464-0 • Original Price: $55
Market Value: $55

222

Williamsburg House
Issued: 1985 • Retired: 1988
#5046-6 • Original Price: $37
Market Value: $152

223

Woodbury House
Issued: 1993 • Retired: 1996
#5444-5 • Original Price: $45
Market Value: $67

224

Wooden Church
Issued: 1983 • Retired: 1985
#5031-8 • Original Price: $30
Market Value: $350

225

Wooden Clapboard
Issued: 1981 • Retired: 1984
#5072-5 • Original Price: $32
Market Value: $248

SNOW VILLAGE
– BUILDINGS –

	Year Purchased	Price Paid	Value Of My Collection
220.			
221.			
222.			
223.			
224.			
225.			
PENCIL TOTALS			

SNOW VILLAGE ACCESSORIES

With the addition of 22 new accessories for 1999, Snow Village holds the record for having the most pieces of any Department 56 collection. So far, there have been 183 accessories released since 1979. The most valuable accessory is "Scottie With Tree," which currently commands a market value of over $200.

1

3 Nuns With Songbooks
Issued: 1987 • Retired: 1988
#5102-0 • Orig. Price: $6
Market Value: $138

2 *New!*

1955 Ford® Automobiles (6 assorted)
Issued: 1998 • Current
#54950 • Orig. Price: $10 (ea.)
Market Value: $10 (ea.)

3 *New!*

1964½ Ford® Mustang (3 assorted)
Issued: 1998 • Current
#54951 • Orig. Price: $10 (ea.)
Market Value: $10 (ea.)

4 *New!*

. . . Another Man's Treasure Accessories (set/3)
Issued: 1998 • Current
#54976 • Orig. Price: $27.50
Market Value: $27.50

5

Apple Girl/Newspaper Boy (set/2)
Issued: 1988 • Retired: 1990
#5129-2 • Orig. Price: $11
Market Value: $28

6

At The Barn Dance, It's Allemande Left (set/2)
Issued: 1997 • Current
#54929 • Orig. Price: $30
Market Value: $30

7   Version 1   Version 2

Auto With Tree
Issued: 1985 • Current
#5055-5 • Orig. Price: $5
Market Value: 1 – $80 (short/flat) 2 – $6.50 (tall/round)

SNOW VILLAGE – ACCESSORIES –

	Year Purch.	Price Paid	Value Of My Collection
1.			
2.			
3.			
4.			
5.			
6.			
7.			
PENCIL TOTALS			

SNOW VILLAGE – ACCESSORIES –

⑧ New!

Biplane Up In The Sky
Issued: 1998 • Current
#52731 • Orig. Price: $50
Market Value: $50

⑨

Bringing Home The Tree
Issued: 1989 • Retired: 1992
#5169-1 • Orig. Price: $15
Market Value: $33

⑩

Calling All Cars (set/2)
Issued: 1989 • Retired: 1991
#5174-8 • Orig. Price: $15
Market Value: $68

⑪

Carnival Tickets & Cotton Candy
Issued: 1998 • Current
#54938 • Orig. Price: $30
Market Value: $30

⑫

Carolers (set/4)
Issued: 1979 • Retired: 1986
#5064-1 • Orig. Price: $12
Market Value: $122

⑬

Caroling At The Farm
Issued: 1994 • Current
#5463-1 • Orig. Price: $35
Market Value: $35

⑭

Caroling Family (set/3)
Issued: 1987 • Retired: 1990
#5105-5 • Orig. Price: $20
Market Value: $37

⑮

Caroling Through The Snow
Issued: 1996 • Current
#54896 • Orig. Price: $15
Market Value: $15

⑯ New!

The Catch Of The Day
Issued: 1998 • Current
#54956 • Orig. Price: $30
Market Value: $30

SNOW VILLAGE – ACCESSORIES –

	Year Purch.	Price Paid	Value Of My Collection
8.			
9.			
10.			
11.			
12.			
13.			
14.			
15.			
16.			
PENCIL TOTALS			

17

Ceramic Car
Issued: 1980 • Retired: 1986
#5069-0 • Orig. Price: $5
Market Value: $62

18

Ceramic Sleigh
Issued: 1981 • Retired: 1986
#5079-2 • Orig. Price: $5
Market Value: $68

19

Check It Out
Bookmobile (set/3)
Issued: 1993 • Retired: 1995
#5451-8 • Orig. Price: $25
Market Value: $40

20

Children In Band
Issued: 1987 • Retired: 1989
#5104-7 • Orig. Price: $15
Market Value: $38

21

Choir Kids
Issued: 1989 • Retired: 1992
#5147-0 • Orig. Price: $15
Market Value: $34

22

Chopping Firewood
(set/2)
Issued: 1995 • Current
#54863 • Orig. Price: $16.50
Market Value: $16.50

23

Christmas At The Farm
(set/2)
Issued: 1993 • Retired: 1996
#5450-0 • Orig. Price: $16
Market Value: $26

24

Christmas Cadillac
Issued: 1991 • Retired: 1994
#5413-5 • Orig. Price: $9
Market Value: $22

25

Christmas Children
(set/4)
Issued: 1987 • Retired: 1990
#5107-1 • Orig. Price: $20
Market Value: $38

26

Christmas Kids (set/5)
Issued: 1997 • Current
#54922 • Orig. Price: $27.50
Market Value: $27.50

SNOW VILLAGE
— ACCESSORIES —

	Year Purch.	Price Paid	Value Of My Collection
17.			
18.			
19.			
20.			
21.			
22.			
23.			
24.			
25.			
26.			
PENCIL TOTALS			

**SNOW VILLAGE
— ACCESSORIES —**

(27)

Christmas Puppies (set/2)
Issued: 1992 • Retired: 1996
#5432-1 • Orig. Price: $27.50
Market Value: $40

(28)

Christmas Trash Cans (set/2)
Issued: 1990 • Retired: 1998
#5209-4 • Orig. Price: $6.50
Market Value: $9

(29)
New!

Christmas Visit To The Florist (set/3)
Issued: 1998 • Current
#54957 • Orig. Price: $30
Market Value: $30

(30)

Classic Cars (set/3)
Issued: 1993 • Retired: 1998
#5457-7 • Orig. Price: $22.50
Market Value: $25

(31)

Coca-Cola® Brand Billboard
Issued: 1994 • Retired: 1997
#5481-0 • Orig. Price: $18
Market Value: $26

(32)

Coca-Cola® Brand Delivery Men (set/2)
Issued: 1994 • Retired: 1998
#5480-1 • Orig. Price: $25
Market Value: $31

SNOW VILLAGE – ACCESSORIES –

	Year Purch.	Price Paid	Value Of My Collection
27.			
28.			
29.			
30.			
31.			
32.			
33.			
34.			
35.			
PENCIL TOTALS			

(33)

Coca-Cola® Brand Delivery Truck
Issued: 1994 • Retired: 1998
#5479-8 • Orig. Price: $15
Market Value: $22

(34)

Cold Weather Sports (set/4)
Issued: 1991 • Retired: 1994
#5410-0 • Orig. Price: $27.50
Market Value: $50

(35)

Snow Village
PARADE

Come Join The Parade
Issued: 1991 • Retired: 1992
#5411-9 • Orig. Price: $12.50
Market Value: $25

(36) New!

Costumes For Sale (set/2)
Issued: 1998 • Current
#54973 • Orig. Price: $60
Market Value: $60

(37) New!

Couldn't Wait Until Christmas
Issued: 1998 • Current
#54972 • Orig. Price: $17
Market Value: $17

(38)

Country Harvest
Issued: 1991 • Retired: 1993
#5415-1 • Orig. Price: $13
Market Value: $32

(39)

Crack The Whip (set/3)
Issued: 1989 • Retired: 1996
#5171-3 • Orig. Price: $25
Market Value: $34

(40)

Doghouse/Cat In Garbage Can (set/2)
Issued: 1988 • Retired: 1992
#5131-4 • Orig. Price: $15
Market Value: $30

(41)

Down The Chimney He Goes
Issued: 1990 • Retired: 1993
#5158-6 • Orig. Price: $6.50
Market Value: $19

(42)

Early Morning Delivery (set/3)
Issued: 1992 • Retired: 1995
#5431-3 • Orig. Price: $27.50
Market Value: $38

(43)

Everybody Goes Skating At Rollerama (set/2)
Issued: 1997 • Current
#54928 • Orig. Price: $25
Market Value: $25

(44) Version 1   Version 2

Family Mom/Kids, Goose/Girl (set/2)
Issued: 1985 • Retired: 1988
#5057-1 • Orig. Price: $11
Market Value: 1 – $55 (large) 2 – $47 (small)

SNOW VILLAGE – ACCESSORIES –

	Year Purch.	Price Paid	Value Of My Collection
36.			
37.			
38.			
39.			
40.			
41.			
42.			
43.			
44.			
PENCIL TOTALS			

SNOW VILLAGE – ACCESSORIES –

(45)

Farm Accessory Set (set/35)
Issued: 1997 • Current
#54931 • Orig. Price: $75
Market Value: $75

(46) *New!*

Farmer's Flatbed
Issued: 1998 • Current
#54955 • Orig. Price: $17.50
Market Value: $17.50

(47)

Feeding The Birds (set/3)
Issued: 1994 • Retired: 1997
#5473-9 • Orig. Price: $25
Market Value: $29

(48)

Fire Hydrant And Mailbox (set/2)
Issued: 1988 • Retired: 1998
#5132-2 • Orig. Price: $6
Market Value: $9

(49) *New!*

Fireman To The Rescue (set/3)
Issued: 1998 • Current
#54953 • Orig. Price: $30
Market Value: $30

(50)

Firewood Delivery Truck
Issued: 1995 • Current
#54864 • Orig. Price: $15
Market Value: $15

SNOW VILLAGE
– ACCESSORIES –

	Year Purch.	Price Paid	Value Of My Collection
45.			
46.			
47.			
48.			
49.			
50.			
51.			
52.			
53.			
PENCIL TOTALS			

(51)

First Round Of The Year (set/3, track compatible)
Issued: 1998 • Current
#54936 • Orig. Price: $30
Market Value: $30

(52)

Flag Pole
Issued: 1989 • Current
#5177-2 • Orig. Price: $8.50
Market Value: $8.50

(53)

Version 1 HOUSE FOR SALE

Version 2

For Sale Sign
Issued: 1987 • Retired: 1989
#5108-0 • Orig. Price: $3.50
Market Value:
1 – $12 (general release) *2 – $20 (blank sign, #581-9)*

54 Version 1   Version 2

For Sale Sign
Issued: 1989 • Retired: 1998
#5166-7 • Orig. Price: $4.50
Market Value: **1** *– $7 (general release)*
2 – $23 (1990 Bachman's Village Gathering Sign)

55

Fresh Frozen Fish (set/2)
Issued: 1990 • Retired: 1993
#5163-2 • Orig. Price: $20
Market Value: $43

56

Frosty Playtime (set/3)
Issued: 1995 • Retired: 1997
#54860 • Orig. Price: $30
Market Value: $38

57
New!

**Fun At The Firehouse
(set/2)**
Issued: 1998 • Current
#54954 • Orig. Price: $27.50
Market Value: $27.50

58

**Girl/Snowman, Boy
(set/2)**
Issued: 1986 • Retired: 1987
#5095-4 • Orig. Price: $11
Market Value: $70

59

**Going To The
Chapel (set/2)**
Issued: 1994 • Current
#5476-3 • Orig. Price: $20
Market Value: $20

60

Grand Ole Opry Carolers
Issued: 1995 • Retired: 1997
#54867 • Orig. Price: $25
Market Value: $29

61

**Harley-Davidson®
Fat Boy & Softail**
Issued: 1996 • Current
#54900 • Orig. Price: $16.50
Market Value: $17.50

SNOW VILLAGE
– ACCESSORIES –

	Year Purch.	Price Paid	Value Of My Collection
54.			
55.			
56.			
57.			
58.			
59.			
60.			
61.			
PENCIL TOTALS			

SNOW VILLAGE
– ACCESSORIES –

62

**A Harley-Davidson®
Holiday (set/2)**
Issued: 1996 • Current
#54898 • Orig. Price: $22.50
Market Value: $25

63

Harley-Davidson® Sign
Issued: 1996 • Current
#54901 • Orig. Price: $18
Market Value: $18

64
New!

**Harley-Davidson®
Water Tower**
Issued: 1998 • Current
#54975 • Orig. Price: $32.50
Market Value: $32.50

65

Hayride
Issued: 1988 • Retired: 1990
#5117-9 • Orig. Price: $30
Market Value: $66

66

**He Led Them Down The
Streets Of Town (set/3)**
Issued: 1997 • Current
#54927 • Orig. Price: $30
Market Value: $30

67

**Heading For The Hills
(2 assorted)**
Issued: 1996 • Current
#54897 • Orig. Price: $8.50 (ea.)
Market Value: $8.50 (ea.)

68

A Heavy Snowfall (set/2)
Issued: 1992 • Current
#5434-8 • Orig. Price: $16
Market Value: $16

69

**A Herd Of Holiday Heifers
(set/3)**
Issued: 1993 • Retired: 1997
#5455-0 • Orig. Price: $18
Market Value: $28

**SNOW VILLAGE
– ACCESSORIES –**

	Year Purch.	Price Paid	Value Of My Collection
62.			
63.			
64.			
65.			
66.			
67.			
68.			
69.			
PENCIL TOTALS			

70

**Here Comes Santa
(LE-1996)**
Issued: 1996 • Retired: 1996
Various • Orig. Price: $25
*Market Value:
all exclusives – $42
(Fortunoff – $80)*

Bachman's (#07744), Bronner's
(#07745), Broughton (#07748),
Cabbage Rose (#07752), Calabash
(#07753), Calico Butterfly (#07751),
Carson Pirie Scott (#07763),
Christmas Loft (#07755), Dickens
Gift Shop (#07750), European
Imports (#07762), Fibber Magee's
(#07747), Fortunoff (#07741),
Gustaf's (#07759), Ingle's Nook
(#07754), Limited Edition (#07746),
North Pole City (#07742), Pine Cone
(#07740), Royal Dutch (#07760),
Russ Country Gardens (#07756), St.
Nick's (#07757), Seventh Avenue
(#07758), Stats (#07749), William
Glen (#07743), Young's Ltd. (#07761)

71

**Here We Come A Caroling
(set/3)**
Issued: 1990 • Retired: 1992
#5161-6 • Orig. Price: $18
Market Value: $30

72

**Hitch Up The Buckboard
(track compatible)**
Issued: 1997 • Current
#54930 • Orig. Price: $40
Market Value: $40

73

Holiday Hoops (set/3)
Issued: 1996 • Current
#54893 • Orig. Price: $20
Market Value: $20

74

**A Holiday Sleigh
Ride Together
(track compatible)**
Issued: 1997 • Current
#54921 • Orig. Price: $32.50
Market Value: $32.50

75

Home Delivery (set/2)
Issued: 1990 • Retired: 1992
#5162-4 • Orig. Price: $16
Market Value: $40

76

**A Home For
The Holidays**
Issued: 1990 • Retired: 1996
#5165-9 • Orig. Price: $6.50
Market Value: $12

77

Just Married (set/2)
Issued: 1995 • Current
#54879 • Orig. Price: $25
Market Value: $25

	SNOW VILLAGE – ACCESSORIES –		
	Year Purch.	Price Paid	Value Of My Collection
70.			
71.			
72.			
73.			
74.			
75.			
76.			
77.			
PENCIL TOTALS			

SNOW VILLAGE
– ACCESSORIES –

(78) Version 1   Version 2

Kids Around The Tree
Issued: 1986 • Retired: 1990
#5094-6 • Orig. Price: $15
Market Value: **1** – $62 *(large)* **2** – $48 *(small)*

(79)

Kids, Candy Canes . . . And Ronald McDonald® (set/3)
Issued: 1997 • Current
#54926 • Orig. Price: $30
Market Value: $30

(80)

Kids Decorating The Village Sign
Issued: 1990 • Retired: 1993
#5134-9 • Orig. Price: $12.50
Market Value: $29

(81)

**Kids Love Hershey's™!
(set/2)**
Issued: 1997 • Current
#54924 • Orig. Price: $30
Market Value: $30

(82)

Kids Tree House
Issued: 1989 • Retired: 1991
#5168-3 • Orig. Price: $25
Market Value: $60

SNOW VILLAGE
— ACCESSORIES —

	Year Purch.	Price Paid	Value Of My Collection
78.			
79.			
80.			
81.			
82.			
83.			
84.			
85.			
86.			

PENCIL TOTALS

(83)

**Let It Snow, Let It Snow
(track compatible)**
Issued: 1997 • Current
#54923 • Orig. Price: $20
Market Value: $20

(84)

U.S. MAIL

Mailbox
Issued: 1989 • Retired: 1990
#5179-9 • Orig. Price: $3.50
Market Value: $22

(85)

MAIL

Mailbox
Issued: 1990 • Retired: 1998
#5198-5 • Orig. Price: $3.50
Market Value: $6

(86)

**Man On Ladder
Hanging Garland**
Issued: 1988 • Retired: 1992
#5116-0 • Orig. Price: $7.50
Market Value: $21

(87)

Marshmallow Roast (set/3)
Issued: 1994 • Current
#5478-0 • Orig. Price: $32.50
Market Value: $32.50

(88)

McDonald's® . . . Lights Up The Night
Issued: 1997 • Current
#54925 • Orig. Price: $30
Market Value: $30

(89)

Men At Work (set/5)
Issued: 1996 • Retired: 1998
#54894 • Orig. Price: $27.50
Market Value: $30

(90)

Monks-A-Caroling
Issued: 1983 • Retired: 1984
#6459-9 • Orig. Price: $6
Market Value: $68

(91)

Monks-A-Caroling
Issued: 1984 • Retired: 1988
#5040-7 • Orig. Price: $6
Market Value: $52

(92)

Moving Day (set/3)
Issued: 1996 • Retired: 1998
#54892 • Orig. Price: $32.50
Market Value: $36

(93)

Mush! (set/2)
Issued: 1994 • Retired: 1997
#5474-7 • Orig. Price: $20
Market Value: $25

(94)

Nanny And The Preschoolers (set/2)
Issued: 1992 • Retired: 1994
#5430-5 • Orig. Price: $27.50
Market Value: $42

(95)

Nativity
Issued: 1988 • Current
#5135-7 • Orig. Price: $7.50
Market Value: $7.50

(96)

On The Road Again (set/2)
Issued: 1996 • Current
#54891 • Orig. Price: $20
Market Value: $20

SNOW VILLAGE – ACCESSORIES –

	Year Purch.	Price Paid	Value Of My Collection
87.			
88.			
89.			
90.			
91.			
92.			
93.			
94.			
95.			
96.			
PENCIL TOTALS			

SNOW VILLAGE – ACCESSORIES –

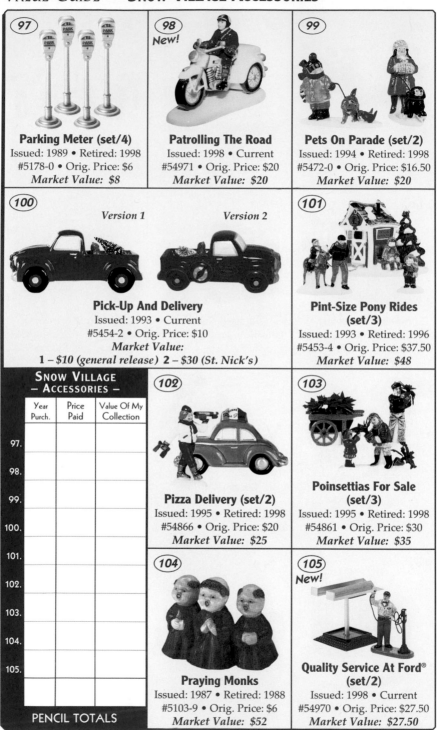

(97)

Parking Meter (set/4)
Issued: 1989 • Retired: 1998
#5178-0 • Orig. Price: $6
Market Value: $8

(98)
New!

Patrolling The Road
Issued: 1998 • Current
#54971 • Orig. Price: $20
Market Value: $20

(99)

Pets On Parade (set/2)
Issued: 1994 • Retired: 1998
#5472-0 • Orig. Price: $16.50
Market Value: $20

(100)

Version 1   *Version 2*

Pick-Up And Delivery
Issued: 1993 • Current
#5454-2 • Orig. Price: $10
Market Value:
1 – $10 (general release) **2 – $30 (St. Nick's)**

(101)

Pint-Size Pony Rides (set/3)
Issued: 1993 • Retired: 1996
#5453-4 • Orig. Price: $37.50
Market Value: $48

(102)

Pizza Delivery (set/2)
Issued: 1995 • Retired: 1998
#54866 • Orig. Price: $20
Market Value: $25

(103)

Poinsettias For Sale (set/3)
Issued: 1995 • Retired: 1998
#54861 • Orig. Price: $30
Market Value: $35

(104)

Praying Monks
Issued: 1987 • Retired: 1988
#5103-9 • Orig. Price: $6
Market Value: $52

(105)
New!

Quality Service At Ford® (set/2)
Issued: 1998 • Current
#54970 • Orig. Price: $27.50
Market Value: $27.50

SNOW VILLAGE — ACCESSORIES —		
	Year Purch.	Price Paid	Value Of My Collection
97.			
98.			
99.			
100.			
101.			
102.			
103.			
104.			
105.			
PENCIL TOTALS			

(106)

**A Ride On The
Reindeer Lines (set/3)**
Issued: 1996 • Retired: 1997
#54875 • Orig. Price: $35
Market Value: $43

(107)

**Round And Round We
Go! (set/2)**
Issued: 1992 • Retired: 1995
#5433-0 • Orig. Price: $18
Market Value: $31

(108)

Safety Patrol (set/4)
Issued: 1993 • Retired: 1997
#5449-6 • Orig. Price: $27.50
Market Value: $32

(109)

**Santa Comes To
Town, 1995 (LE-1995)**
Issued: 1994 • Retired: 1995
#5477-1 • Orig. Price: $30
Market Value: $45

(110)

**Santa Comes To
Town, 1996 (LE-1996)**
Issued: 1995 • Retired: 1996
#54862 • Orig. Price: $32.50
Market Value: $43

(111)

**Santa Comes To
Town, 1997 (LE-1997)**
Issued: 1996 • Retired: 1997
#54899 • Orig. Price: $35
Market Value: $43

(112)

**Santa Comes To
Town, 1998 (LE-1998)**
Issued: 1997 • Retired: 1998
#54920 • Orig. Price: $30
Market Value: $33

(113)
New!

**Santa Comes To Town,
1999 (LE-1999)**
Issued: 1998 • Current
#54958 • Orig. Price: $30
Market Value: $30

(114)   Version 1   Version 2

Santa/Mailbox (set/2)
Issued: 1985 • Retired: 1988
#5059-8 • Orig. Price: $11
Market Value: 1 – $59 (large) 2 – $56 (small)

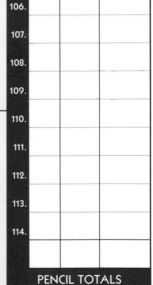

	SNOW VILLAGE – ACCESSORIES –		
	Year Purch.	Price Paid	Value Of My Collection
106.			
107.			
108.			
109.			
110.			
111.			
112.			
113.			
114.			
PENCIL TOTALS			

SNOW VILLAGE – ACCESSORIES –

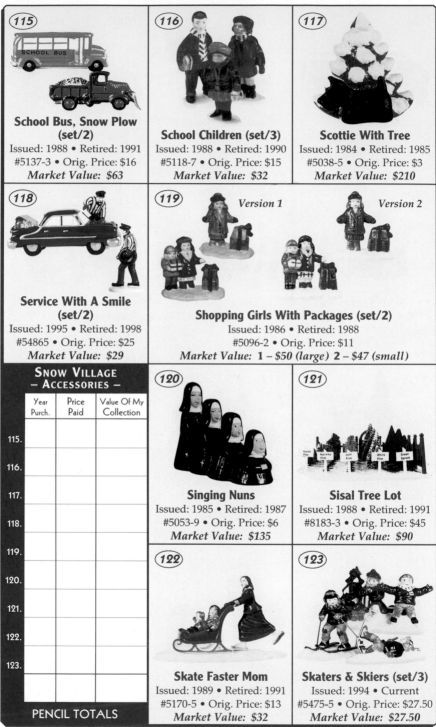

(115)

School Bus, Snow Plow (set/2)
Issued: 1988 • Retired: 1991
#5137-3 • Orig. Price: $16
Market Value: $63

(116)

School Children (set/3)
Issued: 1988 • Retired: 1990
#5118-7 • Orig. Price: $15
Market Value: $32

(117)

Scottie With Tree
Issued: 1984 • Retired: 1985
#5038-5 • Orig. Price: $3
Market Value: $210

(118)

Service With A Smile (set/2)
Issued: 1995 • Retired: 1998
#54865 • Orig. Price: $25
Market Value: $29

(119) *Version 1*   *Version 2*

Shopping Girls With Packages (set/2)
Issued: 1986 • Retired: 1988
#5096-2 • Orig. Price: $11
Market Value: 1 – $50 (large) 2 – $47 (small)

SNOW VILLAGE – ACCESSORIES –

	Year Purch.	Price Paid	Value Of My Collection
115.			
116.			
117.			
118.			
119.			
120.			
121.			
122.			
123.			
PENCIL TOTALS			

(120)

Singing Nuns
Issued: 1985 • Retired: 1987
#5053-9 • Orig. Price: $6
Market Value: $135

(121)

Sisal Tree Lot
Issued: 1988 • Retired: 1991
#8183-3 • Orig. Price: $45
Market Value: $90

(122)

Skate Faster Mom
Issued: 1989 • Retired: 1991
#5170-5 • Orig. Price: $13
Market Value: $32

(123)

Skaters & Skiers (set/3)
Issued: 1994 • Current
#5475-5 • Orig. Price: $27.50
Market Value: $27.50

(124)
New!

Ski Slope
Issued: 1998 • Current
#52733 • Orig. Price: $75
Market Value: $75

(125)

Sleighride
Issued: 1990 • Retired: 1992
#5160-8 • Orig. Price: $30
Market Value: $62

(126)

Sno-Jet Snowmobile
Issued: 1990 • Retired: 1993
#5159-4 • Orig. Price: $15
Market Value: $30

(127)

Snow Carnival Ice Sculptures (set/2)
Issued: 1995 • Retired: 1998
#54868 • Orig. Price: $27.50
Market Value: $32

(128)

Snow Carnival King & Queen
Issued: 1995 • Retired: 1998
#54869 • Orig. Price: $35
Market Value: $40

(129)

Snow Kids (set/4)
Issued: 1987 • Retired: 1990
#5113-6 • Orig. Price: $20
Market Value: $57

(130)

Snow Kids Sled, Skis (set/2)
Issued: 1985 • Retired: 1987
#5056-3 • Orig. Price: $11
Market Value: $54

(131)

Snow Village Promotional Sign
Issued: 1989 • Retired: 1990
#9948-1 • Orig. Price: N/A
Market Value: $24

(132)

Snowball Fort (set/3)
Issued: 1991 • Retired: 1993
#5414-3 • Orig. Price: $27.50
Market Value: $42

(133)

Snowman With Broom
Issued: 1982 • Retired: 1990
#5018-0 • Orig. Price: $3
Market Value: $13

SNOW VILLAGE – ACCESSORIES –

	Year Purch.	Price Paid	Value Of My Collection
124.			
125.			
126.			
127.			
128.			
129.			
130.			
131.			
132.			
133.			
PENCIL TOTALS			

SNOW VILLAGE – ACCESSORIES –

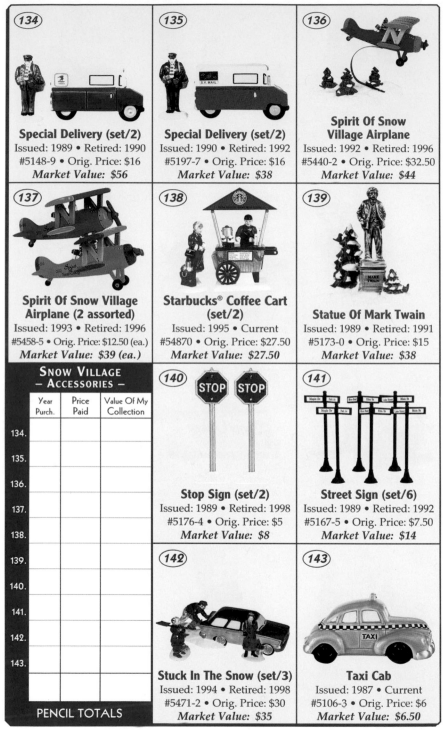

134

Special Delivery (set/2)
Issued: 1989 • Retired: 1990
#5148-9 • Orig. Price: $16
Market Value: $56

135

Special Delivery (set/2)
Issued: 1990 • Retired: 1992
#5197-7 • Orig. Price: $16
Market Value: $38

136

Spirit Of Snow Village Airplane
Issued: 1992 • Retired: 1996
#5440-2 • Orig. Price: $32.50
Market Value: $44

137

Spirit Of Snow Village Airplane (2 assorted)
Issued: 1993 • Retired: 1996
#5458-5 • Orig. Price: $12.50 (ea.)
Market Value: $39 (ea.)

138

Starbucks® Coffee Cart (set/2)
Issued: 1995 • Current
#54870 • Orig. Price: $27.50
Market Value: $27.50

139

Statue Of Mark Twain
Issued: 1989 • Retired: 1991
#5173-0 • Orig. Price: $15
Market Value: $38

SNOW VILLAGE
– ACCESSORIES –

	Year Purch.	Price Paid	Value Of My Collection
134.			
135.			
136.			
137.			
138.			
139.			
140.			
141.			
142.			
143.			
PENCIL TOTALS			

140

Stop Sign (set/2)
Issued: 1989 • Retired: 1998
#5176-4 • Orig. Price: $5
Market Value: $8

141

Street Sign (set/6)
Issued: 1989 • Retired: 1992
#5167-5 • Orig. Price: $7.50
Market Value: $14

142

Stuck In The Snow (set/3)
Issued: 1994 • Retired: 1998
#5471-2 • Orig. Price: $30
Market Value: $35

143

Taxi Cab
Issued: 1987 • Current
#5106-3 • Orig. Price: $6
Market Value: $6.50

(144)

Terry's Towing (set/2)
Issued: 1996 • Current
#54895 • Orig. Price: $20
Market Value: $20

(145)

Through The Woods (set/2)
Issued: 1989 • Retired: 1991
#5172-1 • Orig. Price: $18
Market Value: $33

(146)

Tour The Village
Issued: 1993 • Retired: 1997
#5452-6 • Orig. Price: $12.50
Market Value: $21

(147)

A Tree For Me (set/2)
Issued: 1990 • Retired: 1995
#5164-0 • Orig. Price: $7.50
Market Value: $15

(148)

Tree Lot
Issued: 1988 • Current
#5138-1 • Orig. Price: $33.50
Market Value: $37.50

(149)

Treetop Tree House
Issued: 1996 • Current
#54890 • Orig. Price: $35
Market Value: $36.50

(150)

Trick-Or-Treat Kids (set/3)
Issued: 1998 • Current
#54937 • Orig. Price: $33
Market Value: $33

(151)

Two For The Road (track compatible)
Issued: 1998 • Current
#54939 • Orig. Price: $20
Market Value: $20

(152)
New!

Uncle Sam's Fireworks Stand (set/2)
Issued: 1998 • Current
#54974 • Orig. Price: $45
Market Value: $45

(153)

Up On A Roof Top
Issued: 1988 • Current
#5139-0 • Orig. Price: $6.50
Market Value: $6.50

SNOW VILLAGE — ACCESSORIES —

	Year Purch.	Price Paid	Value Of My Collection
144.			
145.			
146.			
147.			
148.			
149.			
150.			
151.			
152.			
153.			
PENCIL TOTALS			

SNOW VILLAGE — ACCESSORIES —

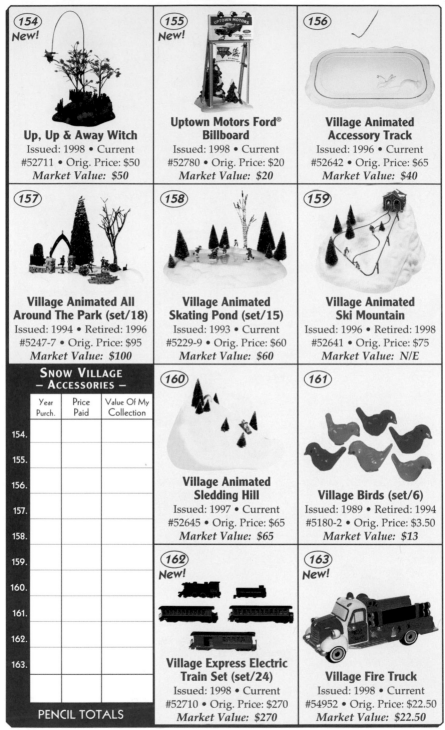

154 New!

Up, Up & Away Witch
Issued: 1998 • Current
#52711 • Orig. Price: $50
Market Value: $50

155 New!

**Uptown Motors Ford®
Billboard**
Issued: 1998 • Current
#52780 • Orig. Price: $20
Market Value: $20

156

**Village Animated
Accessory Track**
Issued: 1996 • Current
#52642 • Orig. Price: $65
Market Value: $40

157

**Village Animated All
Around The Park (set/18)**
Issued: 1994 • Retired: 1996
#5247-7 • Orig. Price: $95
Market Value: $100

158

**Village Animated
Skating Pond (set/15)**
Issued: 1993 • Current
#5229-9 • Orig. Price: $60
Market Value: $60

159

**Village Animated
Ski Mountain**
Issued: 1996 • Retired: 1998
#52641 • Orig. Price: $75
Market Value: N/E

SNOW VILLAGE
— ACCESSORIES —

	Year Purch.	Price Paid	Value Of My Collection
154.			
155.			
156.			
157.			
158.			
159.			
160.			
161.			
162.			
163.			
PENCIL TOTALS			

160

**Village Animated
Sledding Hill**
Issued: 1997 • Current
#52645 • Orig. Price: $65
Market Value: $65

161

Village Birds (set/6)
Issued: 1989 • Retired: 1994
#5180-2 • Orig. Price: $3.50
Market Value: $13

162 New!

**Village Express Electric
Train Set (set/24)**
Issued: 1998 • Current
#52710 • Orig. Price: $270
Market Value: $270

163 New!

Village Fire Truck
Issued: 1998 • Current
#54952 • Orig. Price: $22.50
Market Value: $22.50

164

Village Gazebo
Issued: 1989 • Retired: 1995
#5146-2 • Orig. Price: $27
Market Value: $47

165

Village Greetings (set/3)
Issued: 1991 • Retired: 1994
#5418-6 • Orig. Price: $5
Market Value: $10

166

Village Marching Band (set/3)
Issued: 1991 • Retired: 1992
#5412-7 • Orig. Price: $30
Market Value: $64

167

Village News Delivery (set/2)
Issued: 1993 • Retired: 1996
#5459-3 • Orig. Price: $15
Market Value: $26

168

Village Phone Booth
Issued: 1992 • Current
#5429-1 • Orig. Price: $7.50
Market Value: $7.50

169

Village Potted Topiary Pair
Issued: 1989 • Retired: 1994
#5192-6 • Orig. Price: $5
Market Value: $13

170 New!

Village Service Vehicles (set/3, track compatible)
Issued: 1998 • Current
#54959 • Orig. Price: $45
Market Value: $45

171

Village Streetcar (set/10)
Issued: 1994 • Retired: 1998
#5240-0 • Orig. Price: $65
Market Value: N/E

172

Village Up, Up & Away, Animated Sleigh
Issued: 1995 • Current
#52593 • Orig. Price: $40
Market Value: $40

173

Village Used Car Lot (set/5)
Issued: 1992 • Retired: 1997
#5428-3 • Orig. Price: $45
Market Value: $55

SNOW VILLAGE – ACCESSORIES

	Year Purch.	Price Paid	Value Of My Collection
164.			
165.			
166.			
167.			
168.			
169.			
170.			
171.			
172.			
173.			
PENCIL TOTALS			

SNOW VILLAGE – ACCESSORIES –

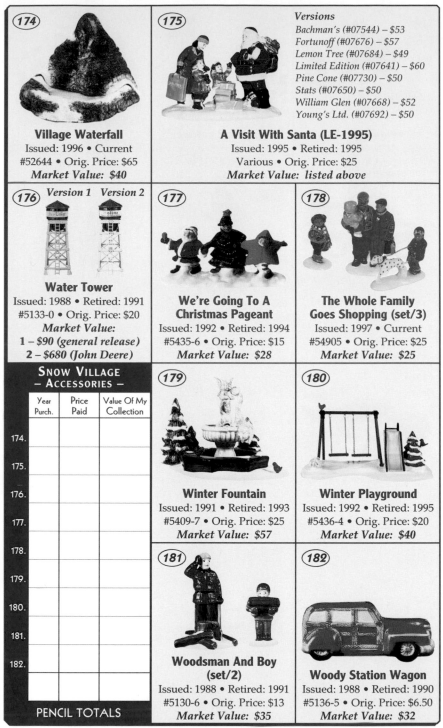

(174)

Village Waterfall
Issued: 1996 • Current
#52644 • Orig. Price: $65
Market Value: $40

(175)

A Visit With Santa (LE-1995)
Issued: 1995 • Retired: 1995
Various • Orig. Price: $25
Market Value: listed above

Versions
Bachman's (#07544) – $53
Fortunoff (#07676) – $57
Lemon Tree (#07684) – $49
Limited Edition (#07641) – $60
Pine Cone (#07730) – $50
Stats (#07650) – $50
William Glen (#07668) – $52
Young's Ltd. (#07692) – $50

(176) Version 1   Version 2

Water Tower
Issued: 1988 • Retired: 1991
#5133-0 • Orig. Price: $20
Market Value:
1 – $90 (general release)
2 – $680 (John Deere)

(177)

We're Going To A Christmas Pageant
Issued: 1992 • Retired: 1994
#5435-6 • Orig. Price: $15
Market Value: $28

(178)

The Whole Family Goes Shopping (set/3)
Issued: 1997 • Current
#54905 • Orig. Price: $25
Market Value: $25

SNOW VILLAGE
— ACCESSORIES —

	Year Purch.	Price Paid	Value Of My Collection
174.			
175.			
176.			
177.			
178.			
179.			
180.			
181.			
182.			
PENCIL TOTALS			

(179)

Winter Fountain
Issued: 1991 • Retired: 1993
#5409-7 • Orig. Price: $25
Market Value: $57

(180)

Winter Playground
Issued: 1992 • Retired: 1995
#5436-4 • Orig. Price: $20
Market Value: $40

(181)

Woodsman And Boy (set/2)
Issued: 1988 • Retired: 1991
#5130-6 • Orig. Price: $13
Market Value: $35

(182)

Woody Station Wagon
Issued: 1988 • Retired: 1990
#5136-5 • Orig. Price: $6.50
Market Value: $32

183

Wreaths For Sale (set/4)
Issued: 1991 • Retired: 1994
#5408-9 • Orig. Price: $27.50
Market Value: $47

SNOW VILLAGE ORNAMENTS

This year, five lighted ornaments join the *Classic Ornament Series* for Snow Village.

1

J. Young's Granary
Classic Ornament Series
Issued: 1997 • Retired: 1998
#98632 • Orig. Price: $15
Market Value: $17

2
New!

J. Young's Granary
Classic Ornament Series
Issued: 1998 • Current
#98644 • Orig. Price: $20
Market Value: $20

3
New!

Lighthouse
Classic Ornament Series
Issued: 1998 • Current
#98635 • Orig. Price: $20
Market Value: $20

4

Nantucket
Classic Ornament Series
Issued: 1997 • Retired: 1998
#98630 • Orig. Price: $15
Market Value: $17

5
New!

Nantucket
Classic Ornament Series
Issued: 1998 • Current
#98642 • Orig. Price: $20
Market Value: $20

6
New!

Pinewood Log Cabin
Classic Ornament Series
Issued: 1998 • Current
#98637 • Orig. Price: $20
Market Value: $20

7

Steepled Church
Classic Ornament Series
Issued: 1997 • Retired: 1998
#98631 • Orig. Price: $15
Market Value: $17

8
New!

Steepled Church
Issued: 1998 • Current
#98643 • Orig. Price: $20
Market Value: $20

SNOW VILLAGE – ACCESSORIES –		
Year Purch.	Price Paid	Value Of My Collection
183.		

SNOW VILLAGE – ORNAMENTS –		
1.		
2.		
3.		
4.		
5.		
6.		
7.		
8.		
PENCIL TOTALS		

SNOW VILLAGE – ACCESSORIES/ORNAMENTS –

187

VALUE GUIDE — FUTURE RELEASES

Use this page to record future Snow Village releases.

SNOW VILLAGE	Original Price	Status	Market Value	Year Purch.	Price Paid	Value Of My Collection
PENCIL TOTALS						

TOTAL VALUE OF MY COLLECTION

Record the value of your collection here by adding the pencil totals from the bottom of each Value Guide page.

SNOW VILLAGE BUILDINGS

Page Number	Price Paid	Market Value
Page 133		
Page 134		
Page 135		
Page 136		
Page 137		
Page 138		
Page 139		
Page 140		
Page 141		
Page 142		
Page 143		
Page 144		
Page 145		
Page 146		
Page 147		
Page 148		
Page 149		
Page 150		
Page 151		
Page 152		
Page 153		
Page 154		
Page 155		
Page 156		
Page 157		
Page 158		
Page 159		
Page 160		
Page 161		
Page 162		
Page 163		
Page 164		
Page 165		
Page 166		
TOTAL		

SNOW VILLAGE ACCESSORIES

Page Number	Price Paid	Market Value
Page 167		
Page 168		
Page 169		
Page 170		
Page 171		
Page 172		
Page 173		
Page 174		
Page 175		
Page 176		
Page 177		
Page 178		
Page 179		
Page 180		
Page 181		
Page 182		
Page 183		
Page 184		
Page 185		
Page 186		
Page 187		
TOTAL		

SNOW VILLAGE ORNAMENTS

Page Number	Price Paid	Market Value
Page 187		
TOTAL		

GRAND TOTALS

	PRICE PAID	MARKET VALUE

*B*eyond the exciting worlds of Heritage Village and Snow Village, there are several other interesting village collectibles by Department 56. Have a look:

SEASONS BAY

Introduced this year, Seasons Bay is the latest village to join the distinctive Department 56 collection. This refreshing new line captures life as it was at the turn of the century. Seasons Bay depicts a small resort town and features lightly colored buildings where vacationers can dine, shop and relax.

This exciting collection allows collectors the freedom of creating a springtime garden scene, a summer scene at the beach, as well as fall and winter displays. Part of this is because the pewter accessories (this is the first time pewter has been used for a Department 56 village) are designed specifically for each season of the year.

Also new for a Department 56 village is the issuing of editions in the Seasons Bay line. First editions of these new pieces will only be available at Gold Key Dealers, while the following edition will be available to Showcase Dealers, as well as Gold Key Dealers. Each edition will have slight changes in color and design and first edition pieces will have a special decal. First and second edition pieces will also have separate stock numbers.

STORYBOOK VILLAGE

Storybook Village, a Department 56 village introduced in 1996, is a fun and inventive line geared toward the child in all of us. All pieces are based on classic nursery rhymes and the buildings are usually sold as a set with their appropriate accessories. This collection experienced its first retirements at the end of 1998.

OTHER COLLECTIBLES

Attending the Bachman's Village Gathering in Minneapolis has become a tradition for some Department 56 collectors and each year the event features several exclusive pieces. In 1998, one building and two accessories were available. The "Bachman Greenhouse" is a lighted building that complements the previous year's event piece, "Bachman's Flower Shop." The greenhouse made its way into the Snow Village general line this year under a different name, "The Secret Garden Greenhouse." Also, "Tending The Cold Frame," one of the event accessories, made its way into the general *Dickens' Village* line. "Say It With Flowers" is the only one of the three pieces issued solely for the Bachman's event.

The Profile Series is a series containing buildings licensed to specific companies. There are only three buildings in this series to date; two of which are retired. The third piece makes its debut in 1999. The pieces are available first to employees of the company and then a limited quantity is made available to collectors. So far, Heinz and State Farm have participated in this special series.

Several other pieces have come and gone from Department 56 without ever "joining" a village. *Meadowland* was introduced in 1979 and retired in 1980, with only two buildings and two sets of accessories. The *Bachman's Hometown Series* also lasted just one year. It was introduced in 1987 and retired with just three buildings.

So far, two Canadian Exclusives have been introduced by Department 56. The first was the "Village Express Van," released in 1992, followed by a lighted building, the "Canadian Trading Co.," in 1997.

*S*ix buildings and 14 accessories make their debut in the new Seasons Bay collection, while three new pieces are added to Storybook Village. Two more new releases that have not been assigned to a specific village will be available at a special Department 56 event in July.

SEASONS BAY

GRANDVIEW SHORES HOTEL . . . Collectors won't believe their eyes when they see this magnificent hotel. The grandeur is evident even in the tiniest of details, from the tower on the rooftop, to the doors that welcome guests. The first edition piece has a weather vane on the clock tower and gold flags on the roof peaks. The regular edition will not have the weather vane and will have different flags.

BAY STREET SHOPS (SET/2) . . . "Book Nook and Bayside Clothiers" and "Maggie's Millinery" offer visitors a day of shopping. Window shopping is a must as the season's fashions hang from many of the windows, while the latest best-sellers are stacked in others. The first edition of this piece will feature gold flags and a decal. There will be color changes to the flags and no decal on the regular edition piece.

CHAPEL ON THE HILL . . . Seasons Bay has become a popular spot for young couples in love and "Chapel On The Hill" is where it all begins. Beautiful weddings are held throughout the year, as well as Sunday morning worship services. The gold cross on the rooftop and decal signify a first edition piece.

SIDE PORCH CAFÉ . . . It doesn't take long to work up an appetite while taking in the sights of Seasons Bay. And there's no place better than the "Side Porch Café" for a meal, whether it's a quick sandwich or a gourmet dinner featuring the chef's specialties. The first edition of this piece has a decal.

WHAT'S NEW FOR OTHER DEPARTMENT 56 COLLECTIBLES

INGLENOOK COTTAGE #5 . . . This is just one of the cottages at Seasons Bay that offers guests a place to relax without the busy atmosphere of a hotel. "Inglenook Cottage #5" has a front porch from which guests can watch the sun set, a bay window with a small deck on top and a fireplace for those extra cold nights. The first edition of this piece has a decal.

THE GRAND CREAMERY . . . Every vacation spot needs an ice cream store and "The Grand Creamery" is Seasons Bay's. If the uniqueness of the structure (half round and half square) isn't reason enough to draw visitors inside, the different flavors of ice cream are sure to do the trick. The first edition of this piece has a decal and a gold flag on the roof. The flag on the regular edition will have a color change and no decal.

SEASONS BAY SPRING ACCESSORIES . . . It's obvious that spring has arrived in Seasons Bay, with children **"RELAXING IN A GARDEN"** (set/3) and a mother and her baby taking **"A STROLL IN THE PARK"** (set/5). **"I'M WISHING"** shows a little boy gazing into a wishing well. A family is on their way to spend **"SUNDAY MORNING AT THE CHAPEL"** (set/2), while a local boy rides his horse, which is pulling **"THE GARDEN CART."**

SEASONS BAY SUMMER ACCESSORIES . . . Signs of summer are all around as a young boy goes **"FISHING IN THE BAY."** An ice cream cart tempts two children in **"HERE COMES THE ICE CREAM MAN"** (set/4) and other children wave flags, anxiously awaiting the **"4TH OF JULY PARADE"** (set/5). **"A DAY AT THE WATERFRONT"** (set/2) captures a mother resting in her beach chair, while two children build a castle in the sand.

SEASONS BAY FALL ACCESSORIES . . . Fall means busy days at the produce stands. That's why a young boy riding his horse pulls a cart **"BACK FROM THE ORCHARD."** And fall also means that everyone in Seasons Bay can't wait to dress up for Halloween and **"TRICK OR TREAT"** (set/4).

What's New For Other Department 56 Collectibles

SEASONS BAY WINTER ACCESSORIES . . . A couple enjoys the sights on an **"AFTERNOON SLEIGH RIDE."** Other visitors enjoy spending their time **"SKATING ON THE POND"** (set/2) or just having **"FUN IN THE SNOW"** (set/2).

STORYBOOK VILLAGE

H.D. DIDDLE FIDDLES (SET/4) . . . The cow is indeed jumping over the moon in this portrayal of the favorite nursery rhyme. The front door is in the middle of the fiddle, which makes up most of the front of the building, while the fiddle's bow stands as a lamppost. Two jesters complement the piece, along with the cat and dog, and of course, cow.

AN OLD HOUSE IN PARIS THAT WAS COVERED WITH VINES (SET/9) . . . This adorable set of nine comes from the popular story of *Madeline*, in celebration of the book's 60th anniversary. As the name implies, this house has been completely taken over by vines. Bright lamps shine on both sides of the building, while five school girls and their instructor head outside with a dog close behind.

P. PETER'S (SET/3) . . . The home of Peter, Peter Pumpkin Eater is blooming with business. On one side of the house made of a pumpkin is an office with a sign for "Marriage Counseling," while on the other is another sign that says "Pumpkin Pies." The roof looks just like the top of a pumpkin still in the patch, complete with the stalk and vine.

MISCELLANEOUS

INDEPENDENCE HALL (SET/2) . . . This grand structure (which hasn't been assigned to a specific collection within Heritage Village) becomes the first piece in the *Historical Landmark Series* to feature a building not based in England.

STARS AND STRIPES FOREVER . . . This Heritage Village accessory is a music box that has been specifically released for this July's Department 56 event.

OTHER DEPARTMENT 56 COLLECTIBLES

This section highlights pieces that are "special" to Department 56. Included are licensed buildings designed for specific companies, exclusives, event and Canadian pieces, as well as the recently released "Collectors' Club House." Also included is the new "Seasons Bay" collection.

1

Hometown Boarding House
Issued: 1987 • Retired: 1988
#670-0 • Orig. Price: $34
Market Value: $325

2

Hometown Church
Issued: 1987 • Retired: 1988
#671-8 • Orig. Price: $40
Market Value: $360

3

Hometown Drugstore
Issued: 1988 • Retired: 1989
#672-6 • Orig. Price: $40
Market Value: $585

4

Countryside Church
Issued: 1979 • Retired: 1980
#5051-8 • Orig. Price: $25
Market Value: $650

5

Thatched Cottage
Issued: 1979 • Retired: 1980
#5050-0 • Orig. Price: $30
Market Value: $690

6

Aspen Trees
Issued: 1979 • Retired: 1980
#5052-6 • Orig. Price: $16
Market Value: $365

7

Sheep (set/12)
Issued: 1979 • Retired: 1980
#5053-4 • Orig. Price: $12
Market Value: $295

8

New!

Bay Street Shops (set/2, First Edition)
Issued: 1998 • Current
#53301 • Orig. Price: $135
Market Value: $135

	BACHMAN'S HOMETOWN SERIES		
	Year Purch.	Price Paid	Value Of My Collection
1.			
2.			
3.			
	MEADOWLAND		
4.			
5.			
6.			
7.			
	SEASONS BAY – BUILDINGS –		
8.			
	PENCIL TOTALS		

OTHER COLLECTIBLES

9
New!

Bay Street Shops (set/2)
Issued: 1998 • Current
#53401 • Orig. Price: $135
Market Value: $135

10
New!

**Chapel On The Hill
(First Edition)**
Issued: 1998 • Current
#53302 • Orig. Price: $72
Market Value: $72

11
New!

Chapel On The Hill
Issued: 1998 • Current
#53402 • Orig. Price: $72
Market Value: $72

12
New!

**The Grand Creamery
(First Edition)**
Issued: 1998 • Current
#53305 • Orig. Price: $60
Market Value: $60

13
New!

The Grand Creamery
Issued: 1998 • Current
#53405 • Orig. Price: $60
Market Value: $60

14
New!

**Grandview Shores Hotel
(First Edition)**
Issued: 1998 • Current
#53300 • Orig. Price: $150
Market Value: $150

SEASONS BAY
— BUILDINGS —

	Year Purch.	Price Paid	Value Of My Collection
9.			
10.			
11.			
12.			
13.			
14.			
15.			
16.			
17.			
18.			

PENCIL TOTALS

15
New!

Grandview Shores Hotel
Issued: 1998 • Current
#53400 • Orig. Price: $150
Market Value: $150

16
New!

**Inglenook Cottage #5
(First Edition)**
Issued: 1998 • Current
#53304 • Orig. Price: $60
Market Value: $60

17
New!

Inglenook Cottage #5
Issued: 1998 • Current
#53404 • Orig. Price: $60
Market Value: $60

18
New!

**Side Porch Café
(First Edition)**
Issued: 1998 • Current
#53303 • Orig. Price: $50
Market Value: $50

All Seasons Bay buildings shown are First Editions. Subsequent editions may vary.

(19) New!

Side Porch Café
Issued: 1998 • Current
#53403 • Orig. Price: $50
Market Value: $50

(20) New!

The Garden Cart
Issued: 1998 • Current
#53327 • Orig. Price: $27.50
Market Value: $27.50

(21) New!

I'm Wishing
Issued: 1998 • Current
#53309 • Orig. Price: $13
Market Value: $13

(22) New!

**Relaxing In A Garden
(set/3)**
Issued: 1998 • Current
#53307 • Orig. Price: $25
Market Value: $25

(23) New!

**A Stroll In The Park
(set/5)**
Issued: 1998 • Current
#53308 • Orig. Price: $25
Market Value: $25

(24) New!

**Sunday Morning At
The Chapel (set/2)**
Issued: 1998 • Current
#53311 • Orig. Price: $17
Market Value: $17

(25) New!

4th Of July Parade (set/5)
Issued: 1998 • Current
#53317 • Orig. Price: $32.50
Market Value: $32.50

(26) New!

**A Day At The Waterfront
(set/2)**
Issued: 1998 • Current
#53326 • Orig. Price: $20
Market Value: $20

(27) New!

Fishing In The Bay
Issued: 1998 • Current
#53313 • Orig. Price: $13
Market Value: $13

(28) New!

**Here Comes The Ice
Cream Man (set/4)**
Issued: 1998 • Current
#53314 • Orig. Price: $35
Market Value: $35

SEASONS BAY – BUILDINGS –

	Year Purch.	Price Paid	Value Of My Collection
19.			

SEASONS BAY – SPRING ACCESSORIES –

20.			
21.			
22.			
23.			
24.			

SEASONS BAY – SUMMER ACCESSORIES –

25.			
26.			
27.			
28.			

PENCIL TOTALS

OTHER COLLECTIBLES

29 New!

Back From The Orchard
Issued: 1998 • Current
#53320 • Orig. Price: $27.50
Market Value: $27.50

30 New!

Trick Or Treat (set/4)
Issued: 1998 • Current
#53319 • Orig. Price: $25
Market Value: $25

31 New!

Afternoon Sleigh Ride
Issued: 1998 • Current
#53322 • Orig. Price: $27.50
Market Value: $27.50

32 New!

Fun In The Snow (set/2)
Issued: 1998 • Current
#53323 • Orig. Price: $15
Market Value: $15

33 New!

Skating On The Pond (set/2)
Issued: 1998 • Current
#53324 • Orig. Price: $20
Market Value: $20

34

Goldilocks Bed And Breakfast (set/4)
Issued: 1996 • Current
#13193 • Orig. Price: $95
Market Value: $75

35 New!

H.D. Diddle Fiddles (set/4)
Issued: 1998 • Current
#13183 • Orig. Price: $75
Market Value: $75

36

Hickory Dickory Dock (set/3)
Issued: 1996 • Retired: 1998
#13195 • Orig. Price: $95
Market Value: N/E

37

Humpty Dumpty Café (set/4)
Issued: 1997 • Current
#13181 • Orig. Price: $95
Market Value: $75

38

Lambsville School (set/5)
Issued: 1996 • Current
#13194 • Orig. Price: $95
Market Value: $75

SEASONS BAY – FALL ACCESSORIES –

	Year Purch.	Price Paid	Value Of My Collection
29.			
30.			

SEASONS BAY – WINTER ACCESSORIES –

31.			
32.			
33.			

STORYBOOK VILLAGE

34.			
35.			
36.			
37.			
38.			

PENCIL TOTALS

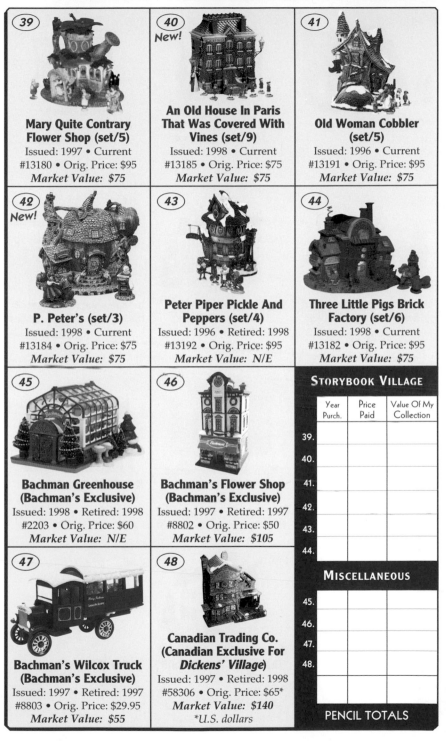

39

Mary Quite Contrary Flower Shop (set/5)
Issued: 1997 • Current
#13180 • Orig. Price: $95
Market Value: $75

40 New!

An Old House In Paris That Was Covered With Vines (set/9)
Issued: 1998 • Current
#13185 • Orig. Price: $75
Market Value: $75

41

Old Woman Cobbler (set/5)
Issued: 1996 • Current
#13191 • Orig. Price: $95
Market Value: $75

42 New!

P. Peter's (set/3)
Issued: 1998 • Current
#13184 • Orig. Price: $75
Market Value: $75

43

Peter Piper Pickle And Peppers (set/4)
Issued: 1996 • Retired: 1998
#13192 • Orig. Price: $95
Market Value: N/E

44

Three Little Pigs Brick Factory (set/6)
Issued: 1998 • Current
#13182 • Orig. Price: $95
Market Value: $75

45

Bachman Greenhouse (Bachman's Exclusive)
Issued: 1998 • Retired: 1998
#2203 • Orig. Price: $60
Market Value: N/E

46

Bachman's Flower Shop (Bachman's Exclusive)
Issued: 1997 • Retired: 1997
#8802 • Orig. Price: $50
Market Value: $105

47

Bachman's Wilcox Truck (Bachman's Exclusive)
Issued: 1997 • Retired: 1997
#8803 • Orig. Price: $29.95
Market Value: $55

48

Canadian Trading Co. (Canadian Exclusive For *Dickens' Village*)
Issued: 1997 • Retired: 1998
#58306 • Orig. Price: $65*
Market Value: $140
*U.S. dollars

STORYBOOK VILLAGE

	Year Purch.	Price Paid	Value Of My Collection
39.			
40.			
41.			
42.			
43.			
44.			

MISCELLANEOUS

45.			
46.			
47.			
48.			
PENCIL TOTALS			

OTHER COLLECTIBLES

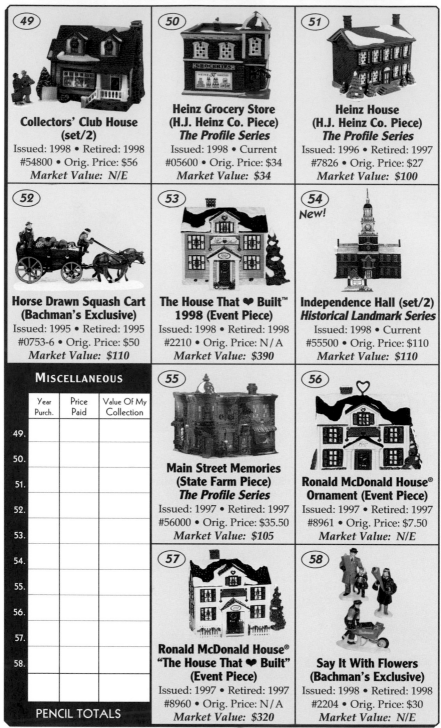

(49)

Collectors' Club House (set/2)
Issued: 1998 • Retired: 1998
#54800 • Orig. Price: $56
Market Value: N/E

(50)

Heinz Grocery Store (H.J. Heinz Co. Piece)
The Profile Series
Issued: 1998 • Current
#05600 • Orig. Price: $34
Market Value: $34

(51)

Heinz House (H.J. Heinz Co. Piece)
The Profile Series
Issued: 1996 • Retired: 1997
#7826 • Orig. Price: $27
Market Value: $100

(52)

Horse Drawn Squash Cart (Bachman's Exclusive)
Issued: 1995 • Retired: 1995
#0753-6 • Orig. Price: $50
Market Value: $110

(53)

The House That ♥ Built™ 1998 (Event Piece)
Issued: 1998 • Retired: 1998
#2210 • Orig. Price: N/A
Market Value: $390

(54)
New!

Independence Hall (set/2)
Historical Landmark Series
Issued: 1998 • Current
#55500 • Orig. Price: $110
Market Value: $110

MISCELLANEOUS

	Year Purch.	Price Paid	Value Of My Collection
49.			
50.			
51.			
52.			
53.			
54.			
55.			
56.			
57.			
58.			

PENCIL TOTALS

(55)

Main Street Memories (State Farm Piece)
The Profile Series
Issued: 1997 • Retired: 1997
#56000 • Orig. Price: $35.50
Market Value: $105

(56)

Ronald McDonald House® Ornament (Event Piece)
Issued: 1997 • Retired: 1997
#8961 • Orig. Price: $7.50
Market Value: N/E

(57)

Ronald McDonald House® "The House That ♥ Built" (Event Piece)
Issued: 1997 • Retired: 1997
#8960 • Orig. Price: N/A
Market Value: $320

(58)

Say It With Flowers (Bachman's Exclusive)
Issued: 1998 • Retired: 1998
#2204 • Orig. Price: $30
Market Value: N/E

59 New!

Stars And Stripes Forever (Event Piece)
Issued: 1998 • Current
#55502 • Orig. Price: $50
Market Value: $50

60

Tending The Cold Frame (Bachman's Exclusive)
Issued: 1998 • Retired: 1998
#2208 • Orig. Price: $35
Market Value: N/E

61

Village Express Van (Canadian Exclusive For Heritage Village)
Issued: 1992 • Retired: 1996
#5865-3 • Orig. Price: $25*
Market Value: $70
U.S. dollars

	MISCELLANEOUS		
	Year Purch.	Price Paid	Value Of My Collection
59.			
60.			
61.			
PENCIL TOTALS			

OTHER COLLECTIBLES

VALUE GUIDE — FUTURE RELEASES/TOTAL VALUE OF MY COLLECTION

Use this page to record future Department 56 releases.

OTHER DEPARTMENT 56 COLLECTIBLES	Original Price	Status	Market Value	Year Purch.	Price Paid	Value Of My Collection
				PENCIL TOTALS		

Record the value of your collection here by adding the pencil totals from the bottom of each Value Guide page.

OTHER DEPARTMENT 56 COLLECTIBLES		
Page Number	Price Paid	Market Value
Page 195		
Page 196		
Page 197		
TOTAL		

OTHER DEPARTMENT 56 COLLECTIBLES		
Page Number	Price Paid	Market Value
Page 198		
Page 199		
Page 200		
Page 201		
TOTAL		

GRAND TOTALS		
	PRICE PAID	MARKET VALUE

*A*s your Department 56 collection grows, you may wonder where to turn to find the pieces that are no longer in production. While there is a possibility that you may find some of these elusive pieces at a garage sale or hidden in the back room of your favorite retailer, you're much more likely to find them on the secondary market.

The secondary market is a meeting ground where collectors can buy, sell and trade items (including rare pieces that can be nearly impossible to find). However, before one dives into the secondary market, it is wise to understand how it functions and what to expect.

RETIREMENTS

The secondary market for Department 56 was created in 1979 when the company announced the first Snow Village retirements, ensuring the line's status as a collectible. Since then, retirements for all of the villages have been announced annually by Department 56. The announcement is made every year through a large ad in *USA Today*. The information is also posted on the official Department 56 web site. When a piece retires, the mold is broken to ensure that the piece will never be produced again. As retailers' stock of the piece is depleted, demand begins to overtake supply and the piece's value begins to increase, causing the piece to retain what is known as "secondary market value."

LIMITED EDITIONS AND EXCLUSIVES

Popular items on the secondary market include limited edition and exclusive pieces. Limited editions are pieces limited either by production time ("LE-1998") or by the number of pieces produced ("LE-10,000"). Since limited editions often have a smaller production quantity than general releases, retailers are allocated fewer pieces. Some collectors don't have the opportunity to purchase the piece in retail stores, which forces them to look on the secondary market.

Exclusive pieces are those only available through selected retail outlets. This group includes pieces made specifically for certain retailers, such as Fortunoff, and special event pieces, which are only available to collectors attending a specific event. These pieces are often very limited and sell out quickly, leaving the majority of collectors to turn to the secondary market to acquire them.

CONDITION

As with anything else, items that are in the best condition will fetch the highest prices. Stray wisps of paint, chips, cracks and water damage all can reduce the value of a piece on the secondary market. You should inspect each piece carefully before you make your purchase and remember to keep in mind that some pieces on the secondary market have been repaired or restored. It is OK to buy these pieces, as long as you are aware that they will not fetch as high of a resale price.

On the other hand, flawless pieces, or pieces in "mint condition," will fetch the highest amounts on the secondary market. These pieces often have never been removed from their original boxes (or styrofoam packaging and protective sleeve) and are marked on listings as "mint in box" or "MIB." Not only are the boxes important for storage and protection, but pieces sold without their original boxes are often considered "incomplete" and are worth less on the secondary market.

SECONDARY MARKET SOURCES

Your local retailer can be a great resource in your search for elusive pieces. While most retailers are not active on the secondary market, they can often direct you to other collectors in your area who are interesting in buying, selling or trading pieces. In addition, retailers are usually aware of any secondary market shows in your area.

Some of the most active secondary market resources for Department 56 villages are exchange services. For a subscription or membership fee, these services will provide you with a listing of items that collectors are selling, along with the price they are asking. Most services publish these listings weekly or monthly, although some have a daily listing available which can accessed by phone. The service acts as a middleman and often charges a 10% to 20% service fee to complete a transaction.

The Internet has quickly grown to become an important resource for collectors. Bulletin boards welcome posts from collectors who are looking to buy, sell or trade pieces, while auction sites allow for listing and bidding on items. Chat rooms are great places to meet other Department 56 collectors who share the same interests. In addition, many retailers have developed web sites for selling their products on-line.

One last option is to check the classified advertisements of your local newspaper or collectible magazines. Keep in mind, however, that newspapers reach a general audience and may not be as successful as options that are aimed specifically towards collectors.

While the opportunities that the secondary market can bring to your collection are endless, it is important to remember that the secondary market can be unstable. The market fluctuates constantly, so there is no guarantee that values will continue to increase. If you collect Department 56 villages for the monetary investment, you may be disappointed. You're much better off doing it for the fun!

EXCHANGES, DEALERS & NEWSLETTERS

Quarterly
(general information – *a must!*)
Department 56, Inc.
P.O. Box 44056
One Village Place
Eden Prairie, MN 55344-1056
(800) 548-8696

56 Directions
Jeff & Susan McDermott
364 Spring Street Ext.
Glastonbury, CT 06033
(860) 633-8192

Collectible Exchange, Inc.
6621 Columbiana Road
New Middletown, OH 44442
(800) 752-3208

The Cottage Locator
Frank & Florence Wilson
211 No. Bridebrook Rd.
East Lyme, CT 06333
(860) 739-0705

Dickens' Exchange
Lynda W. Blankenship
5150 Highway 22, Suite C-16
Mandeville, LA 70471
(504) 845-1954

Donna's Collectibles Exchange
703 Endeavor Drive South
Winter Springs, FL 32708
(800) 480-5105

*New England Collectibles
Exchange*
Bob Dorman
201 Pine Avenue
Clarksburg, MA 01247
(413) 663-3643

The Village Chronicle
Peter & Jeanne George
757 Park Ave.
Cranston, RI 02910
(401) 467-9343

The Village Press
Roger Bain
P.O. Box 556
Rockford, IL 61105-0556
(815) 965-0901

Villages Classified
Paul & Mirta Burns
P.O. Box 34166
Granada Hills, CA 91394-9166
(818) 368-6765

What The Dickens
Judith Isaacson
2885 West Ribera Place
Tucson, AZ 85742
(520) 297-7019

COLLECTOR'S
VALUE GUIDE™

W hen insuring your collection, there are three major points to consider:

1. KNOW YOUR COVERAGE: Collectibles are typically included in homeowner's or renter's insurance policies. Ask your agent if your policy covers fire, theft, floods, hurricanes, earthquakes and damage or breakage from routine handling. Also, ask if your policy covers claims at "current replacement value" – the amount it would cost to replace items if they were damaged, lost or stolen. This is extremely important since the secondary market value of some pieces may well exceed their original retail price.

2. DOCUMENT YOUR COLLECTION: In the event of a loss, you will need a record of the contents and value of your collection. Ask your insurance agent what information is acceptable. Keep receipts and an inventory of your collection in a different location, such as a safe deposit box. Include the purchase date, price paid, size, issue year, edition, special markings and secondary market value for each piece. Photographs and video footage with close-up views of each piece, including bottomstamps, boxes and signatures, are good back-ups.

3. WEIGH THE RISK: To determine the coverage you need, calculate how much it would cost to replace your collection and compare it to the total amount your current policy would pay. To insure your collection for a specific dollar amount, ask your agent about adding a Personal Articles Floater or a Fine Arts Floater or "rider" to your policy, or insuring your collection under a separate policy. As with all insurance, you must weigh the risk of loss against the cost of additional coverage.

VARIATIONS

*I*n the world of collectibles, change is a common occurrence. And while the release and retirement of pieces in the Department 56 line is to be expected, changes to pieces currently in production are usually unexpected to the public and can often result in a rise in secondary market value. When a change does occur, however, whether it be a change to the mold or a change in color, it is considered to be a "variation." Variations can happen for a variety of reasons. Some variations are the result of corrections to design flaws and are planned by Department 56. Other variations result from subtle (and often accidental) changes in the production process.

One of the more common variations that exists is a change in color. For example, in just four years, there were five different versions of the "Dickens' Village Church." The church, which was originally painted white, began showing up in a cream color shortly after its release. Later, the color was changed to green, tan and, finally, butterscotch. While the first version maintains the highest value on the secondary market due to its limited availability, the others follow closely behind. Another significant color change appears in the "Knob Hill" house inSnow Village. The first version was introduced in 1979 and was off-white with black trim and accents. The second version of this house is bright yellow with white trim.

Color changes are not limited to buildings. The "Small Double Trees" in Snow Village have blue birds on their branches in some versions, while later pieces have red birds. When the "Amish Family" (set/3) in *New England Village* was initially introduced, the man holding the basket was featured with a mustache. Later, Department 56 learned that it is against Amish custom to wear a mustache and the piece was altered so that the man appears with only a beard.

Design changes that affect the mold or construction of a piece are another common variation. "The Flat Of Ebenezer Scrooge" in *Dickens' Village* was released both with gold-colored window panes and without window panes. It has also been noted by some collectors that this piece was manufactured in three different countries. Snow Village's "Train Station With 3 Train Cars" (set/4) also had a design change that involved the piece's windows. The piece first appeared with six window panes on the station and a circular window on the front door. Then, the design was altered to feature eight window panes and two square windows on the front door. Village accessories are not exempt from these types of variations. They too, have experienced mold changes throughout the years. One of the most intriguing is the Snow Village "Auto With Tree." If you were lucky enough to get the first version of this car, you'll notice it has a flat or "squashed" look to it. The current version has a round or "inflated" appearance.

Pieces that have misspelled words appearing on the sleeve or bottomstamp often make for interesting variations. "Kensington Palace," (set/23) which was just recently released, was first found having a misspelled word on its box. While the text should have read "Princess Of Wales," some of the boxes read "Whales" instead. Also, the incorrectly spelled "Seires" has been found on the bottomstamp of "Crooked Fence Cottage" and "Village" was misspelled "Vallage" on the bottomstamp of some "J. Lytes Coal Merchant" pieces.

Princess of Whales.

A series of variations occurred during the mid-1980s that affected many of the Snow Village accessories. For an unknown reason, midway through the life of several pieces their mold was changed to a smaller size than when they were initially introduced. In some instances, there were also minor changes in the appearance of the piece. "Family Mom/Kids, Goose Girl" (set/2) was introduced in 1985 and subsequently retired in 1988, however, at some point in between, the piece was scaled down in size. It also seems as though many of the pieces that underwent this size change became more detailed. To use the "Family Mom/Kids, Goose Girl" (set/2) as an example, if you compare the pieces side-by-side, you will note many changes to the mother's face, hair and coat.

A recent addition to Department 56's normal line-up of releases is the issuing of exclusive pieces. While these are not considered by some to be true variations, they often follow a similar pattern to a piece in the general line, with several design modifications making them a unique addition to any collection. These pieces are usually available from a specific retailer or group.

SO WHAT'S AN ARTIST PROOF?

Prototypes produced in the studios of Department 56 prior to the release of a piece are often used to "test run" various colors, patterns and/or design elements and are called "artist proofs." Although very few are made, on certain occasions they manage to make their way into collectors' hands and become highly valuable on the secondary market.

Even pieces that are exclusive to retailers and have counterparts in the general Department 56 line will have their own proof. For example, the "Lionel® Electric Train Shop," that was released by Allied Model Trains in Culver City, California, is shown top-left. A proof for this exclusive piece is shown below. As you can see, the proof varies slightly from the piece that was actually released. Take a look at the circular windows with the "L" on the front of the building. On the actual piece they are recessed into the brick and feature solid panes, while the arches above the front windows are also filled in. On the 5,000 pieces that were released, the windows and arch do not have panes and the building is a slightly different shade of red.

*C*ountless hours of production go into the creation of each Department 56 building and accessory. Throughout the process, each step is monitored to ensure that Department 56's high standards of quality are evident in every piece.

The process is much the same for Heritage Village and Snow Village, with minor differences due to the different finishes used on the pieces. All village pieces begin on paper, where a drawing is made and used as a guide, or blueprint. The building is then sculpted and from this piece, a mold is made into which "slip," or liquid clay, is poured. The clay is allowed to harden and then is removed from the mold and sanded. The building is now ready for various cosmetic touches, like cutting windows and adding attachments.

When additions are complete, the firing process begins, which takes up to eight hours in a kiln that's heated to at least 1,000 degrees. After the buildings have cooled, they are handpainted. Because Heritage Village pieces have a matte finish, they do not need a coat of glaze, and therefore, only need to be re-fired long enough to dry and set the new paint. Snow Village pieces, however, need to be fired for a longer period of time, and at a higher temperature, to set the top coat of glaze, producing the glossy finish for which they're known.

Department 56 villages are then safely packed in styrofoam and placed in a "sleeve" or box that, beginning this year, has a color picture of the piece on the front. There's also information about the piece and the village on the sleeve. The average price for a Snow Village or Heritage Village building runs between $50 and $100, while accessories are generally $15 to $40. Ornaments are usually around $20, while hinged boxes run between $15 and $25.

C reating the perfect display with your Department 56 buildings and accessories can be a fun and easy project. No matter which village you choose to collect, or what time, space or monetary constraints you may encounter; with a little patience and commitment, you can create a spectacular display of your very own!

THE RIGHT STUFF!

When building a display, the first thing you'll want to do is decide what type of scene you want to create and what, if any, action you would like to take place. Will it be an autumn day of work on the farm, a skating party in the mid-

dle of town or a fishing trip by the shore? Planning in advance will not only help you focus but will provide you with an idea of what accessories and materials you may need to shop for.

Basic necessities to begin your display include: a flat surface to build on, such as a piece of wood or heavy styrofoam, a glue gun, tacky wax, a screwdriver and scissors. Items found around the house and yard like dried moss, pebbles and twigs are also great ways to add authenticity to your display. Food works well, too – cinnamon sticks and peppermints make wonderful sidewalks!

Since most of the villages have a winter or Christmas theme, snow should be one of your main ingredients. There are also many accessories made by Department 56 that are perfect to accentuate any display.

Trees, shrubs, gravel and even a fence can add just the right touch to your display. Also, remember to leave room for lampposts, mailboxes, park benches and people to bring "life" to your display.

LOCATION, LOCATION, LOCATION!

Aside from the decisions to be made on what elements to add to your display, there are also numerous options available as to where to place your village display. The tops of bookshelves, cabinets, and trunks are good, flat surfaces and are usually in a highly visible area – just be sure there is an electrical outlet in sight. While window ledges are very tempting, remember that sun can fade your pieces. If you intend to keep your display up for a long period of time, you may want to think about another location.

JUST MY SIZE!

A large display with multiple buildings and accessories is not the only way to showcase your collection. If you're not very handy with tools, why not spread your collection throughout your home?

Small displays are just as enjoyable and can be placed just about anywhere! Table tops and mantels are two prime locations. Place a building in either spot, then add some

trees and sprinkle snow around the area for a nice, simple display. If you entertain during the holidays, use your buildings and accessories as centerpieces for

THE PERFECT GIFT!

Why not turn a gift for your favorite collector into a display?

All you have to do is fill the bottom of a basket with cotton or another soft filling and set a building on top. Weave ivy around the rim of the basket and up the basket's handle.

Next, add some accessories that suit the theme or style of the building, such as trees, dried leaves (be sure they're clean) or candy.

Your gift is sure to make any collector happy!

the dinner table and if you're setting up your display specifically for Christmas, why not put some buildings right under your Christmas tree? Simply cut back the bottom limbs and place the buildings underneath. Just be careful where you place them so that no sap falls on your buildings. Add a decorative tree skirt and some fresh fallen snow for add further interest. Bookshelves, nightstands and coffee tables are also good places to set up a small vignette.

Since you've worked so hard to build your Department 56 collection, take pride in the displays you build. Then once you're done, sit back and admire your achievement!

*F*or many collectors, the best part of collecting Department 56 villages is working to achieve the perfect display. Using the wide array of accent pieces supplied by Department 56 is a great way to get your display started (see the *Current Display Pieces* section beginning on page 219). As your village grows, a time may come when you just can't find that perfect piece you need to enhance your growing village. So, what can you do? Well, since hiring a general contractor may be a little excessive – why not express your creative side and build custom accessories yourself? Who knows, this could be the start of a great little business to help fund your village hobby.

So, to help those who want to learn step-by-step how to be a "do-it-yourselfer" and for those that are already on their way but are looking for some quick and easy projects; our resident expert, **Dr. S**, provides display shortcuts for two scenic elements – hills and walls – with clear-cut directions.

THE QUICK HILLS

This can be quite messy, but it is also quick and easy!

You will need:
- Lots of newspaper
- Several plastic mixing bowls or small containers
- Small pieces of scrap wood or heavy cardboard
- Plaster or Hydrocal
- Lots of water
- Scraps of fiberglass or aluminum window screening
- Strong paper towels (don't be cheap – this is your hobby)

Display Success With "Dr. S"

Step One: Decide where you want your hills and begin by crumpling newspaper into various size balls. Place the newspapers in the approximate locations of your hills, then step back and see if you like the shapes of the newspaper piles (hereafter called "hills"). Feel free to revise, move papers and get others to give you opinions. If you decide to make your hills higher, you may want to substitute cardboard or wood supports for the newspaper. This will supply stronger support for the plaster.

Step Two: Spread lots of newspapers around the area where you will be working. A small amount of time spent preparing can save much cleanup time later. Spread the screen or another layer of newspaper over your hill contours. Mix the plaster according to the manufacturer's directions. Mix quickly and in small amounts only – this stuff sets fast!

Step Three: Make a pile of separated paper towels and start dipping them in the plaster, one at a time. As you dip into the plaster, move the towel quickly onto the hills. It helps if you sing "The Hills Are Alive With The Sound Of Plaster." Repeat this process until you have a thin layer of plaster-soaked towels covering your hills.

Step Four: Walk away and let the hills dry for 24 hours. If, when you return, you are not sure you like the contours, repeat Steps Two and Three until you are happy with the results.

Step Five: Paint the hills. Before you do this, check your basement or garage for old paint. If you have several partially filled cans of latex, mix them together. Usually the color turns out to be something on the order of drab gray or brown. This is what you want for ground cover. If no old paint is available, go buy some in your local hardware store.

Step Six: While the paint is still wet, sprinkle in some sand and/or ground foam purchased at your local hobby store to add texture and color to the hills. At all times, make sure you look outside your window and keep in mind what hills and vegetation really are like in your area. Once your hills are dry, you may choose to add trees, plaster rock castings, plastic people and all sorts of little details. Much of that material can be purchased from a hobby/model railroad store that sells "0" Gauge (1/48") scale detail parts. That size seems to work well with Department 56 villages. Do experiment and do not be limited by what "should" be done. Remember that this is your world and you are in charge.

THE QUICK WALL

If you want to put a city on two levels, then these walls are for you. They are simple, easy and effective in any size. (You could be truly lazy and just glue brick paper onto foam insulation material, but that is really almost *too* easy.)

You will need:
- Insulating foam, 1" to 2" thick
- Metal ruler, yardstick or meter stick
- Small hobby or utility knife
- Gray latex paint
- Imitation stone spray from a building supply or craft store

Step One: Decide where your retaining walls will be placed. What effect are you trying to achieve? Will the walls separate two levels, or form the basis for a harbor in your town? For this project, we will confine ourselves to the basic granite block wall found all over the eastern United States in railroad abutments, retaining walls and wharves.

Step Two: After you have chosen your location, cut the foam insulation board to size with a utility knife. Do not try to  saw this stuff or you will spend your lifetime picking small pieces of foam from your couch and your cat.

Step Three: Draw parallel horizontal lines across the face of the foam with a felt pen or pencil. The lines should be about 3/8" to 1/2" apart for large granite blocks. Then draw in the vertical lines approximately one inch apart, alternating them just like brick mortar joints. See how easy this is?

Step Four: Place the metal straightedge on the line and lightly score the foam with your hobby knife. Move the metal guide and repeat the process about 1/16" away. This should yield a shallow groove for each mortar joint. Play with this process until you get the look you want – foam is cheap.

Step Five: Paint the wall with gray latex paint. Do not use spray or oil-based paints as they will eat the foam before your very eyes. Two light coats are better than one. You now have a gray chunk of foam.

Step Six: Now that the latex paint has sealed the foam, grab that can of imitation "stone spray" and lightly coat the wall. This should yield a granite-like appearance. You may also use a light India ink wash over the wall and accent with other dark colors. Install your wall and let friends admire it. If you are short on friends when you finish, those little plastic and ceramic people will enjoy it also.

$\mathcal{A}$ great part of the appeal of collecting Department 56 is the creativity of collector's displays. While there are many accessories offered within each collection, Department 56 also offers a plethora of display accessories which can be used to complement the pieces in any of the villages. Some may be designed specifically for Heritage Village, Snow Village or *Dickens' Village* and are identified as (HV), (SV) or (DV). The new issues for 1999 are marked with an asterisk (*).

SNOW
- ❏ Blanket Of New
  Fallen Snow 49956
- ❏ Fresh Fallen Snow
  (7-oz. bag) 49979
- ❏ Fresh Fallen Snow
  (2-lb. box). 49980
- ❏ Real Plastic Snow
  (7-oz. bag) 49981
- ❏ Real Plastic Snow
  (2-lb. box). . . . . , 49999

FENCES
- ❏ Candy Cane Fence 52664
- ❏ Corral Fence. 52746*
- ❏ Halloween Fence
  (set/2) 52702*
- ❏ Snow Fence, White (SV). 52657
- ❏ Twig Snow Fence. 52598
- ❏ Victorian Wrought Iron
  Fence Extension (HV) . 52531
- ❏ Victorian Wrought Iron
  Fence and Gate
  (set/5) (HV) 52523
- ❏ White Picket Fence (SV). 51004
- ❏ Wrought Iron Fence
  (set/4) (HV) 59994

TREES
- ❏ Autumn Birch/Maple
  Tree (set/4) 52655
- ❏ Bare Branch Trees
  (set/6) 52623
- ❏ Bare Branch Tree
  w/25 Lights. 52434
- ❏ Birch Tree Cluster 52631

TREES, cont.
- ❏ Craggy Oak Tree 52748*
- ❏ Decorated Sisal Trees
  (set/2, Asst.) 52714*
- ❏ Flocked Pine Trees
  (set/3) 53367*
- ❏ Frosted Spruce (set/2) . 52637
- ❏ Frosted Topiary (set/2). 52000
- ❏ Frosted Topiary (set/4). 52019
- ❏ Frosted Topiary
  (set/8, Asst. Lg.) 52027
- ❏ Frosted Topiary
  (set/8, Asst. Sm.) 52035
- ❏ Halloween
  Spooky Tree 52770*
- ❏ Holly Tree 52630
- ❏ Jack Pines (set/3) 52622
- ❏ Pine Trees With
  Pine Cones (set/3) 52771*
- ❏ Porcelain Pine
  Trees (set/4) 59001
- ❏ Snowy Evergreen
  Trees, Lg. (set/5) 52614
- ❏ Snowy Evergreen
  Trees, Med. (set/6) 52613
- ❏ Snowy Evergreen
  Trees, Sm. (set/6) 52612
- ❏ Snowy Scotch Pines
  (set/3) 52615
- ❏ Towering Pines (set/2) . 52632
- ❏ Winter Birch (set/6) . . . 52636
- ❏ Winter Pine Trees With
  Pine Cones (set/3) 52772*
- ❏ Wintergreen Pines
  (set/2) 52661
- ❏ Wintergreen Pines
  (set/3) 52660

MISCELLANEOUS ACCENT PIECES

- Acrylic Icicles (set/4) . . 52116
- Bears In The Birch 52743*
- Blue Skies Backdrop . . 52685
- Brick Road (set/2) 52108
- Brick Town Square . . . 52601
- Camden Park
  Cobblestone Road (set/2). 52691
- Camden Park Fountain. 52705*
- Camden Park Square
  (set/21) (DV) 52687
- Camden Park Square
  Stone Wall (DV) 52689
- Candy Cane Bench 52669
- Christmas Eave Trim . . 55115
- Clear Ice 52729*
- Cobblestone Road (set/2). 59846
- Cobblestone Town
  Square. 52602
- Country Road Lamp
  Posts (set/4) 52663
- Fallen Leaves
  (3-oz. bag) 52610
- Fieldstone Entry Gate . 52718*
- Fieldstone Wall
  (3 Asst.) 52717*
- Fieldstone Wall
  With Apple Tree 52768*
- Flexible Autumn
  Hedges (set/2). 52703*
- Flexible Sisal
  Hedge (set/3) 52596
- Flexible Sisal Hedge,
  Lg. (set/3) 52662
- Foxes In The Forest . . . 52744*
- Frosty Light Sprays
  (set/2) 52682
- Gazebo 52652
- Glistening Snow 53362*
- Gray Cobblestone
  Archway 52752*
- Gray Cobblestone
  Capstones (set/2) 52755*
- Grassy Ground Cover
  (3.5-oz. bag) 53347*
- Gravel Road 52756*
- Gray Cobblestone
  Section (set/2). 52751*
- Gray Cobblestone
  Tunnel 52753*
- Green 52739*
- Halloween Set (set/22) . 52704*
- Holiday Tinsel Trims
  (set/11) 52712*
- Holly Split Rail Fence
  (set/4) 52722*

MISCELLANEOUS ACCENT PIECES, cont.

- Holly Split Rail Fence
  With Seated Children . . 52723*
- Hybrid Landscape
  (set/22) 52600
- Landscape (set/14) 52590
- Log Pile 52665
- Magic Smoke
  (6-oz. bottle). 52620
- Mill Creek Bridge 52635
- Mill Creek, Curved
  Section 52634
- Mill Creek Park Bench . 52654
- Mill Creek Pond 52651
- Mill Creek, Straight
  Section 52633
- Mill Creek Wooden
  Bridge 52653
- Moose In The Marsh . . 52742*
- Mountain Backdrop
  (set/2) 5257-4
- Mountain Centerpiece . 52643
- Mountain Tunnel 52582
- Mountain w/
  Frosted Sisal Trees,
  Lg. (set/14). 5228-0
- Mountain w/
  Frosted Sisal Trees,
  Med. (set/8) 5227-2
- Mountain w/
  Frosted Sisal Trees,
  Sm. (set/5) 5226-4
- Mylar Skating
  Pond (set/2) 5208-6
- Peppermint Road,
  Curved Section. 52667
- Peppermint Road,
  Straight Section 52666
- Pine Point Pond 52618
- Pink Flamingos (set/4) . 52595
- Putting Green 52740*
- Railroad Crossing
  Sign (set/2) 55018
- Real Gray Gravel
  (12-oz. bag) 52754*
- Revolving Display
  Stand. 52640
- Road Construction Sign
  (set/2) (SV). 52680
- Slate Stone Path 52719*
- Slate Stone Path 52767*
- Sled & Skis (set/2) 52337
- Starry Night
  Sky Backdrop. 52686
- Stone Curved
  Wall/Bench (set/4) . . . 52650

MISCELLANEOUS ACCENT PIECES, cont.

- ❏ Stone Footbridge 52646
- ❏ Stone Holly Corner
  Posts & Archway (set/3). 52648
- ❏ Stone Holly Tree
  Corner Posts (set/2) ... 52649
- ❏ Stone Stairway 52725*
- ❏ Stone Trestle Bridge... 52647
- ❏ Stone Wall 52629
- ❏ Stone Wall
  With Sisal Hedge 52724*
- ❏ Swinging Under
  The Old Oak Tree..... 52769*
- ❏ Tacky Wax 52175
- ❏ Telephone Poles
  (set/6) (SV).......... 52656
- ❏ Television Antenna
  (set/4) (SV)......... 52658
- ❏ Thoroughbreds (set/5) . 52747*
- ❏ Tinsel Trims (set/8) ... 52713*
- ❏ Two Lane Paved
  Road (SV).......... 52668
- ❏ Village Square
  Clock Tower......... 52591
- ❏ Walkway Lights (set/2). 52681
- ❏ Weather Vane
  (set/5) (SV)......... 52659
- ❏ Windmill (SV) 54569
- ❏ Wolves In The Woods . 52765*
- ❏ Wooden Pier (set/2) ... 52766*
- ❏ Woodland Animals At
  Mill Creek 52720*
- ❏ Wrought Iron
  Park Bench.......... 52302

LIGHTED ACCENT PIECES

- ❏ 6-Socket Light Set 99279
- ❏ 20-Socket Light Set ... 99278
- ❏ 45 LED Light Strand .. 52678
- ❏ AC/DC Adapter 55026
- ❏ Boulevard Lampposts
  (set/4) 52627
- ❏ Carnival Carousel
  LED Light Set 52706*
- ❏ Christmas
  LED Luminaries...... 52715*
- ❏ Double Light Socket
  Adapter............ 99280
- ❏ Double Street Lamps
  (set/4) 59960
- ❏ Fiber Optic Fireworks . 52727*
- ❏ Halloween
  LED Luminaries...... 52738*
- ❏ Jack-O'-Lanterns 52701*
- ❏ LED Light Bulb....... 99247

LIGHTED ACCENT PIECES, cont.

- ❏ Lighted Christmas Pole. 52679
- ❏ Lighted Snowy Tree... 52683
- ❏ Mini Lights
  (set/14 bulbs) 52159
- ❏ Multi-Outlet Plug Strip. 99333
- ❏ Railroad Lamps (set/2). 52760*
- ❏ Replacement
  Light Bulb (set/3)..... 99244
- ❏ Replacement Light
  Bulb, Clear (set/3) 52707*
- ❏ Replacement Light
  Bulb, Yellow (set/3)... 52708*
- ❏ Replacement Round
  Light Bulb (set/3)..... 99245
- ❏ Single Cord Set 99028
- ❏ Spotlight (set/2)....... 52611
- ❏ Spotlight Replacement
  Bulbs (set/6)......... 99246
- ❏ Street Lamps (set/6) 36366
- ❏ String Of 12
  Pumpkin Lights 52700*
- ❏ String Of 25
  Mini LED Lights 52728*
- ❏ String Of Spotlights ... 52779*
- ❏ String Of Starry Lights. 52684
- ❏ Town Tree
  w/50 LED Lights 52639
- ❏ Traffic Light (set/2) ... 55000
- ❏ Turn-Of-The-Century
  Lamppost (set/4) 55042
- ❏ Utility Accessories
  (set/9) (SV).......... 52775*
- ❏ Utility Accessories
  (set/11) (HV) 52776*

VILLAGE BRITE LITES

- ❏ Adapter............. 52256
- ❏ Angel 52671
- ❏ Candles (set/4) 52674
- ❏ Candy Canes (set/2) ... 52670
- ❏ Fence (set/4)......... 52361
- ❏ Holly Archway....... 52675
- ❏ "Merry Christmas".... 52230
- ❏ Reindeer 52248
- ❏ Santa 52396
- ❏ Santa In Chimney..... 52673
- ❏ Snow Dragon 52672
- ❏ Snowman 52370
- ❏ Tree 52388

GLOSSARY

accessory—pieces designed to enhance village buildings. Accessories are typically non-lit miniature figurines.

animated—a piece with motion.

bottomstamp—also called an "understamp," these are identifying marks on the underside of a collectible. Buildings have a bottomstamp which includes the village name, the title of the piece, the copyright date and the Department 56 logo.

exclusive—a piece made especially for, and only available through, a specific store, exposition or buying group.

first edition—pieces with limited production. In Seasons Bay, there will be first edition pieces with a special decal, as well as different colors and attachments than the open edition piece.

collectibles—anything and everything that is "able to be collected," whether it's figurines, dolls . . . or even *watches* can be considered a "collectible," but it is generally recognized that a true collectible should be something that increases in value over time.

Gold Key Dealers—Showcase retailers who are recognized for outstanding commitment to Department 56.

History List—Department 56 promotional material which lists the item number, title, issue year, retail price and retirement year of pieces.

issue date—for Department 56, the year of production is considered the year of "issue," although the piece may not become available to collectors until the following year.

limited edition (LE)—a piece scheduled for a predetermined production quantity or time period.

mid-year introductions—additional Department 56 pieces announced in May. These pieces are usually available in smaller allocations than January introductions at first, but become readily available in subsequent years.

open edition—a piece with no predetermined limitation on time or size of production run.

primary market—the conventional collectibles purchasing process in which collectors buy at issue price through various retail outlets.

release date—the year a piece becomes available to collectors. For most pieces, the release date is the year following the issue date.

retired—a piece which is taken out of production, never to be made again, usually followed by a scarcity of the piece and a rise in value on the secondary market.

secondary market—the source for buying and selling collectibles according to basic supply-and-demand principles ("pay what the market will bear"). Popular pieces, or those that are retired or had low production quantities can appreciate in value far above the original retail price.

series—a grouping within a collection based on a certain theme, such as the *American Architecture Series*.

Showcase Dealers—a select group of retailers who receive early shipments of new and limited edition pieces.

track compatible—pieces that can stand alone, but are made to go with animated tracks.

– Key –

All Heritage and Snow Village pieces are listed below in alphabetical order. The first number refers to the piece's location within the Value Guide section and the second to the box in which it is pictured on that page. Items that are not pictured are listed as "NP."

ALPHABETICAL INDEX

ALPHABETICAL INDEX

ALPHABETICAL INDEX

ACKNOWLEDGEMENTS

CheckerBee Publishing would like to thank Jeff McDermott, Don Sierakowski and Frank Wilson. Also thanks to Lynda Blankenship, Ron Drapeau, Allen Drucker, Linda Hassett, Amy Koosman and all the Department 56 retailers and collectors who contributed their valuable time to assist us with this book. Many thanks to the great people at Department 56.

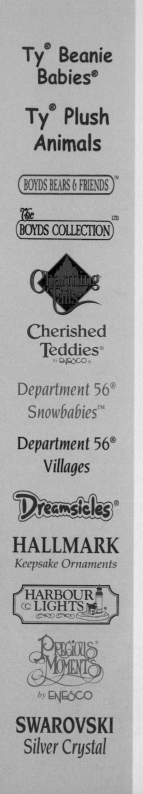